Satan Proof
YOUR HOME

MARILYN HICKEY

CONTENTS

And they overcame him by the blood of the

Lamb, and by the word of their testimony;

and they loved not their lives unto the death.

REVELATION 12:11

CHAPTER ONE

CONSTRUCTING A GODLY HOME

Wouldn't it be wonderful to know that your home was totally secure and not vulnerable to any attack of Satan? We know how bold he can be—why, he'll barge right in without even bothering to knock!

Some people believe that Christians never have struggles, but that's a lie. Satan's not just trying to destroy God's kingdom or the local church—he's after families too! If you haven't taken the precautions for guarding your home against Satan's divisive elements, your family won't withstand the force of his storms. It will crash.

Millions of families are facing failure all over the world. The failure-of-the-family phenomenon indiscriminately reaches into a wide cross section of homes. It ignores race, financial status, and religious preference, and leaves behind a tragic trail of emptiness, bitterness, and despair.

I believe God may have had families in mind when He said, *"My people are destroyed for lack of knowledge . . ."* (Hosea 4:6). Sure, many powerful, demonic forces are contributing to the destruction of the family; some have been undermining the family unit for decades. But, God DID NOT say that we would be destroyed by demonic forces.

Satan is taking advantage of today's family unit because we have fallen prey to one of his most subtle devices—our own lack of knowledge. Paul wrote, *"Lest Satan should get an advantage of us: for we are not ignorant of his devices"* (2 Corinthians 2:11).

I want to teach you how to Satan-proof your home; so that the next time the devil comes near your loved ones, you'll know how to stop him dead in his tracks!

LAY THE RIGHT FOUNDATION

Of course, you cannot effectively stand against the devil on behalf of your loved ones until you have laid the right foundation for Satan-proofing yourself:

Therefore whosoever heareth these sayings of mine, and doeth them, I will liken him unto a wise man, which built his house upon a rock: And the rain descended, and the floods came, and the winds blew, and beat upon that house; and it fell not: for it was founded upon a rock. And every one that heareth these sayings of mine, and doeth them not, shall be likened unto a foolish man, which built his house upon the sand: And the rain descended, and the floods came, and the winds blew, and beat upon that house; and it fell: and great was the fall of it (Matthew 7:24–27).

Your foundation must be built upon a rock. The Bible says Jesus Christ is the rock of our salvation:

And did all drink the same spiritual drink: for they all drank of that spiritual Rock that followed them: and that Rock was Christ (1 Corinthians 10:4).

He shall cry unto me, Thou art my father, my God, and the rock of my salvation (Psalm 89:26).

I receive hundreds of letters each week from people all over the world. Many people write to share the terrible consequences of putting their confidence in something or someone other than Jesus Christ.

One courageous woman shared:

"I was hooked on crack and walked the streets of Daytona Beach collecting aluminum cans to pay for my habit. I lived with crooks, thieves, and prostitutes; and I was all of these. I am an educated woman with a master's degree, and I once had held a $50,000-a-year job. But I did not know Jesus—cocaine was my choice."

Cocaine had become this woman's god, and it almost destroyed her. She eventually was born again, returned to her parents' home, and God began to nurture her back to spiritual health. She had taken the first step to Satan-proofing her home by Satan-proofing herself, and she became a dynamite witness to her family. Since her first letter, her older brother has also been set free from a drug induced lifestyle. He now lives with her, and they are praising the Lord together.

Friends, there absolutely is no question. If you put your hope into anything or anyone less than Jesus, you are building your future on sand and you will fall into destruction.

ERECT A STRONG STRUCTURE

After your eternal life has been established solidly in Christ Jesus, the next step toward Satan-proofing your home is to structure your life on the godly principles contained in God's Word.

My ministry has a Bible reading plan that is excellent! (If you are interested in obtaining a current Bible reading plan, please go to our website at *marilynandsarah.org*.) We receive many testimonies from all kinds of people who have been blessed because they are following our plan and reading through the Bible each year. My heart was so touched when a teenage girl wrote:

"I think it is beneficial for teenagers to read through the Bible. When I first started, it was like I had to make myself read it every day. But once I had established it as a discipline, then it got easier. I don't expect some big revelation every day, I just try to understand what it's really saying . . . and stick with it because in the long road, it will pay off."

This delightful believer's faith has been founded in Jesus Christ, and now she is Satan-proofing herself by studying the Bible. When she is confronted by temptations or trials, her response will be structured by God's Word.

You know, it's curious that BOTH the houses discussed in Matthew 7 were subjected to the same type of storm. I know some of you think your lives automatically became immune to the attacks of the enemy when you were born again. Some of you think your level of spirituality determines whether or not you are attacked by the devil. But it simply isn't so.

Of course, being a mature Christian certainly will give you a tremendous edge over the devil. But the simple fact remains that whether you are a saint or a sinner, a new Christian or a mature believer—Satan will throw his fiery darts at you. Why? Satan hates God; therefore, he also hates people because we were created in God's image:

So God created man in his own image . . . and God said unto them, Be fruitful and multiply, and replenish the earth, and subdue itw (Genesis 1:27–28).

The Hebrew word here for *subdue* means "to tread down, to conquer, to bring into bondage." It's God's will for people to bear fruit, and to control the earth. But first, we must renew our minds and be conformed to the image of Christ (see Romans 12:2; 8:29).

The major thing you will discover as you study your Bible is that Jesus is a winner. And, when you structure your life upon the godly principles that He taught in the Scriptures, YOU will become a winner too!

In Christ, believers have the power to tread over the devil:

Behold, I give unto you power to tread on serpents and scorpions, and over all the power of the enemy: and nothing shall by any means hurt you (Luke 10:19).

In Christ, believers are more than conquerors:

Nay, in all these things we are more than conquerors through him that loved us (Romans 8:37).

In Christ, believers have the authority to bind and loose:

Verily I say unto you, Whatsoever ye shall bind on earth shall be bound in heaven: and whatsoever ye shall loose on earth shall be loosed in heaven (Matthew 18:18).

When you begin to walk fully according to the purpose and in the power given to you by God, you will be able to Satan-proof your home and keep the devil from ripping off your loved ones.

You'll learn to stop listening to the devil's lies! God does not want your marriage to end prematurely because of the death of your spouse or because of divorce. God does not want your family members tormented in relationships that are physically, mentally, emotionally, or sexually abusive. God does not want your family members to fall into sin and become hooked on drugs and alcohol, adultery, pornography, or just plain riotous living. God does not want your finances to be in such turmoil that your family suffers neglect because you must work day and night to make ends meet. NO! He most certainly does not!

God has predestined you, His child, to be conformed into the image of Jesus (see Romans 8:29). Remember, Jesus is a winner; and through Him, you and your family can be winners too!

Although the enemy will try to divide and conquer your household, you can stop him from devastating your lives and Satan-proof your home by taking a stand for your family.

PUT THE WORD INTO ACTION

I noticed something about those two houses in Matthew:

And the rain descended, and the floods came, and the winds blew, and beat upon that house; and it fell not: for it was founded upon a rock (Matthew 7:25).

This first house was Satan-proofed—rooted in Jesus and structured in God's Word. The second house was built on sand (something or someone other than Christ and solid Bible doctrine). Both houses were subjected to the SAME storm; but although the first house may have swayed and bent under the ferocity of the winds and rains—it did not fall. In contrast, the second house had not been Satan-proofed; it had been built on sand. It couldn't handle the pressure of the storm and was destroyed.

Since God wants our families to be Satan-proofed, let's dig deeper into what it takes to be a Satan-proofer. We know without a doubt that being born again is essential and reading the Bible is necessary. But knowing Jesus as our Savior and being aware of godly principles are simply the first steps toward defending our loved ones against Satan's tactics.

Satan-proofers are believers who have taken charge by letting godly principles become alive in their circumstances. They have stepped out of the comfort zone of merely hearing God's Word, into the battle zone of actively doing what God's Word instructs us to do:

But be ye doers of the word, and not hearers only, deceiving your own selves (James 1:22).

The Bible gives us much more than the steps to eternal life; it also provides step-by-step instructions for living in the world every day. When you really get into studying your Bible regularly, you'll be able to Satan-proof your home as you begin to act on the Word of God that is within you. Some people read the Bible over and over again, but fail to apply its divine principles to their everyday lives. The Word has worked for people since Biblical times, and the Word will work in your 21st-century life too!

In order to take a stand upon godly principles, a believer first needs to have developed a trusting relationship with God. Then, when the storms of life come, a Satan-proofer says, "God, I trust You; and I'm going to stand on what Your Word says. I know You are faithful, and You will not fail me."

This type of intimacy between God and man evolves out of a strong, consistent prayer life. A Satan-proofer regularly spends time in God's presence praying, worshipping, praising, fasting, studying, and meditating. A Satan-proofer knows and trusts God to the utmost.

Your relationship with God, based on the rock-solid foundation of Jesus Christ, is what will always hold you steady as you battle the enemy for yourself and your family.

BE A GAP STANDER, NOT A GAP FINDER

Satan-proofing your home requires you to be a gap stander. When I think about standing in the gap for my family, I think about Abraham—he spent time in God's presence and God established a personal relationship with Abraham. I get so encouraged when I look at the relationship between Abraham and God; it was so intimate. The Bible indicates that God even trusted Abraham enough to reveal His plans regarding the coming judgment upon the wicked twin cities of Sodom and Gomorrah:

And the LORD said, Shall I hide from Abraham that thing which I do . . . Because the cry of Sodom and Gomorrah is great, and because their sin is very grievous; I will go down now, and see whether they have done altogether according to the cry of it, which is come unto me; and if not, I will know (Genesis 18:17–21).

These people really were the pits! They were involved in all kinds of things—terrible sexual sins. Some of those awful Sodomite men even demanded that Lot turn over to them the two angels that God had sent to confirm their wicked activities. They wanted to have sex with God's angels—can you say "YUK"? So, God said, "That's enough!" And He destroyed them.

But prior to that, we see God actually conferring with Abraham about His plans to bring judgment upon Sodom and Gomorrah. How did Abraham react? Certainly, he was concerned because Lot and his family lived in Sodom.

Let's see, did Abraham go running to tell Sarah about what God was going to do? Did Abraham start whining to his friends, "Oh, what shall I do? Something awful is going to happen. Please pray for my family." Did Abraham get nervous and start biting his nails or pulling out his hair?

NO! Abraham began to talk with God on behalf of Lot and his family. Abraham began to Satan-proof his family through intercessory prayer:

Peradventure there be fifty righteous within the city: wilt thou also destroy and not spare the place for the fifty righteous that are therein? . . . And the LORD said, If I find in Sodom fifty righteous within the city, then I will spare all the place for their sakes (Genesis 18:24–26).

Abraham kept right on negotiating until God agreed to spare the city even if there were only ten righteous people living in it. Can you imagine, these people were so wicked that it was questionable as to whether Sodom contained ten good people?

I think Abraham probably stopped at ten because he thought there had to be at least ten good people in Sodom. After all, there were six in Lot's family—his wife, two daughters, and their husbands. Abraham had no idea that Lot's two sons-in-law would reject God's offer or that Lot's wife would turn from God too.

Abraham was certain that God would find four more people who had not been overtaken by the terrible sin that was running rampant in that area.

I wonder how I would respond if God suddenly said, "Marilyn, because of the homosexuality, prostitution, and drug abuse in Anywhere, USA; I am going to wipe it off the face of the earth." How would you respond? Some Christians probably would cheer God on and say, "Go ahead, God! We need to get some of these sinners out of here!" But what if you had relatives living in that city, would you feel the same way?

No matter how terrible the place, I believe God would expect us to be merciful and try to save the city if for no other reason than our families are there.

I believe prayer is one way the wise woman in Proverbs 14:1 stood in the gap and Satan-proofed her home. On the other hand, the foolish woman plucked her house down with her own hands. Do you suppose that instead of praying, she just pointed her finger at everyone's mistakes while her family crumbled under the weight of Satan's attacks?

You know, if we took a survey to see whether Christians consider themselves to be gap standers or gap finders, I am reasonably certain that most people probably would answer gap standers! Yet, the heartbreaking statistics on America's failing family structure show that Christian as well as non-Christian families are falling apart.

Friends, this is a cold, hard truth with which we need to come to grips. Most Christians have allowed themselves to become foolish by pointing a finger rather than pointing a prayer. And while we busily have been focusing on the greatness of sin instead of the greatness of God—the devil merrily has been running off with everything we hold dear.

But I want to encourage you—there is hope! It is not too late for Christians to turn this awful trend around and take a stand against the destruction the devil has planned for our families.

God is for families! He doesn't want your family to be destroyed by any of the horrendous things that come out of the devil's devious mind. No, God wants you to become an intercessor and to Satan-proof your family with effective, fervent prayer.

You see, God is omniscient (all-knowing). God knew before He ever shared His plans with Abraham that he would stand in the gap and Satan-proof Lot's family. It didn't matter to Abraham that Lot was a loser, he prayed for him anyway. That's why God allows you to know some not so nice things about your family too. He doesn't want you to point your finger and condemn. Instead, God wants you to pray and stop what the devil is trying to do to your loved ones.

It's up to us to pray for our families—to keep them before God. Who is going to do it if we don't? You say, "Well, I think the church should." But God wants YOU to stand in the gap for your own family.

I just love the way God works when He has gap standers willing to Satan-proof their loved ones.

Abraham could have chosen to be a gap finder and said, "I didn't want Lot to move down there, but he insisted. And Lot didn't just stay out on the plains where he had pitched his tent; he did all his shopping in Sodom, that's where his girls went to school, and he and his wife had an active social life. Why, Lot even sits at the city gate with the other civic leaders. You know, God, he may be family, but Lot really is not so swift. So, go ahead and wipe Sodom out. I'll understand."

Of course, we know Abraham didn't say any of that; instead, he stood in the gap and Satan-proofed Lot and his family with prayer. Abraham didn't think God was going to destroy Sodom and Gomorrah, so imagine how his faith fell when he got up the next morning:

And he looked toward Sodom and Gomorrah, and toward all the land of the plain, and beheld, and, lo, the smoke of the country went up as the smoke of a furnace (Genesis 19:28).

When Abraham saw all that smoke rising, I'm sure he probably thought, "Oh, dear God, dear God, what about Lot? You couldn't find even ten?" Then, sadly, Abraham got discouraged because the outward manifestations of God's answer to his prayer weren't quite what he expected them to be.

It's so easy to become discouraged when we pray and pray for our families. When Wally was alive, he and I prayed for our relatives for years. Some of them got better, but some went from bad to worse.

But I keep praying because God's Word has been formed on the inside of me, and I am holding on to His promises. Abraham let go of God's promises and completely blew it:

And Abraham journeyed from thence toward the south country, and dwelled between Kadesh and Shur, and sojourned in Gerar. And Abraham said of Sarah his wife, She is my sister: and Abimelech king of Gerar sent, and took Sarah. But God came to

Abimelech in a dream by night, and said to him, Behold, thou art but a dead man, for the woman which thou has taken; for she is a man's wife (Genesis 20:1–3).

Abraham was afraid that Lot had been killed. Now, I am sure that many of you have gotten out of whack, too, when things didn't turn out as you thought they should. I certainly have, and like Abraham, I tried to back away from God's plan for my life.

Abraham had gotten out of God's will and into fear. He ended up telling Sarah to lie about being his wife and almost got poor Abimelech killed. Things really got pretty messy for a while until God corrected the situation and put Abraham back on the right track. But if Abraham had not judged God's faithfulness according to his own agenda, he never would have become discouraged and taken this dumb detour down to Gerar anyway.

When we are Satan-proofing our homes, it is important that we not become discouraged and give up just because things don't progress the way we think they should. We have to stick to the Word and believe that God will work His will out in whatever situation our loved ones are facing.

And don't forget the wise woman in Proverbs 14:1—build up rather than tear down. If you keep in mind that the devil is your enemy—never people—you'll never tear your family apart. Rather, you'll always zero in on Satan and tear him apart instead.

Over 50 years ago, before my children were born, my husband Wally, who has now gone to be with Jesus, was severely depressed. He became moody and wouldn't talk to me sometimes for two or three days. I just hated it. I would try to talk to him; but he would say, "I'm a failure. Please don't talk to me.

Don't bother me."

I honestly didn't know what to do. But I heard the Word of God which had formed on the inside of me—that the Holy Spirit will pray for things beyond your understanding. I thought, "I'm going to stop whining around and being mad at Wally. I have the Word inside of me, and I am going to act like the Word works by taking a stand on it."

So, for one hour I prayed in tongues, and God showed me what to do. I sat down and began to go through the scriptures with Wally, reminding him that he could not possibly be a failure because the Bible says that believers will always triumph in Christ.

First Wally just wanted me to leave him alone, but I continued challenging him and insisting that he respond. Finally, he started to laugh and the depression broke.

I stood in the gap and Satan-proofed my home by acting on God's Word inside of me. I spoke the Word, and the devil had to stop attacking my husband with depression.

SPEAK THE WORD OF GOD

The Bible says that God's Word is a sword:

And take the helmet of salvation, and the sword of the Spirit, which is the word of God (Ephesians 6:17).

For the word of God is quick, and powerful, and sharper than any two-edged sword, piercing even to the dividing asunder of soul and spirit, and of the joints and marrow, and is a discerner of the thoughts and intents of the heart (Hebrews 4:12).

Someone once told me about a Spirit-filled man who I'll call

Tom. He had been praying for his sister who was hooked on drugs and involved in all kinds of immorality. She lived a very sinful life. One weekend, while their mother was away, the sister went out and didn't come home until 6:30 the next morning. She brought some athletic-looking guy home with her, and they went into her mother's bedroom.

Tom was almost overwhelmed when he asked God what to do and God told him, "Throw the guy out!" He went into his mother's bedroom, told his sister to put her clothes on, and asked her boyfriend, "How would you feel if your sister brought some guy home to sleep with her in your mother's bed? Would you like it?" The boyfriend responded, "No." Tom told him to get dressed and leave, and the guy did just that. His sister was absolutely furious.

When Tom left and returned to school, he began to Satan-proof his sister. He stood in the gap and spoke FOR his sister saying, "Satan, you can't have any part of my sister. Adultery, you can't have a part of my sister. Drugs, you can't have a part of my sister." Tom continued this for exactly three months, and one day his sister showed up at his door saying, "I want to get saved." The Word of God had cut through all the junk in her life and had turned her completely around!

God's Word discerns the thoughts and intents of the heart. So, when we pray God's Word, using it on spirits and situations, it begins to cut through thoughts and attitudes and brings about a change.

Instead of complaining and allowing corrupt communication (see Ephesians 4:29) to come out of our mouths about how badly people are doing, we literally need to speak to their spirits—by name—"Susie (or whoever), you're not going to drink or take drugs." And then, Satan-proof them by speaking directly to the enemy, "Devil, you're not going to put alcoholism and drug addiction on Susie (or whoever)."

I believe when we begin to speak and continue to speak with persistence to the spirits involved, we will crack some things wide open. Why? Because our foundation is in Jesus—the living Word. The Bible says that we overcome the devil by the blood of the Lamb and the word of our testimony (see Revelation 12:11). We can Satan-proof our loved ones by cutting through some of the garbage in their lives, so they can hear the Holy Spirit; then they will come through with flying colors!

So, you see, it's more than just knowing Jesus and being aware of what God's Word says. A Satan-proofer literally takes the Word and chops the devil's head with it.

Why don't you begin NOW to be wise like the woman in Proverbs 14:1 and build up your loved ones through intercessory prayer?

Women, I believe you can Satan-proof your husbands by speaking the Word over them while you are doing ordinary chores. You could do it while ironing, making the bed, or cooking dinner. Try it by praying, "I thank you, Father, because no weapon formed against my husband shall prosper; and everything that rises against him shall fall." I think something happens in a home when women pray like that; you can prevent violent crimes from occurring in your home and you can put strife on the run!

Men, you can Satan-proof your wife by speaking faith over her and by praying for her. You can say things like, "Mary, you are a mighty woman of God, you have the peace of God that passes all understanding." Speak God's Word concerning obedience into your children's spirits—tell them they will never be rebellious and how smart they are in school because they have the mind of Christ. And then speak with authority to the devil; tell him that he will never get your family because, in the name of Jesus, YOU are standing in the gap for them.

Finally, I cannot emphasize enough the importance of praying in the Holy Spirit. The Bible says:

But ye, beloved, building up yourselves on your most holy faith, praying in the Holy Ghost, Keep yourselves in the love of God, looking for the mercy of our Lord Jesus Christ unto eternal life (Jude 20–21).

Now let me ask you, what do you think would happen if you began to walk around your house praying in the Spirit? Or, on your job? You don't have to make a big fuss, you can pray in the Spirit on the inside—no one would know what you are doing but God.

Praying in the Spirit will keep you in the love of God, and I believe praying in the Spirit will also keep you in love with each other. So, when your spouse, children, or parents get out of line, you will lovingly pray and Satan-proof them. The Holy Spirit will keep you in God's perfect love, and you will act in a way that will bring God's mercy into whatever situation Satan may try to bring against your home.

CHAPTER TWO

PREPARING FOR BATTLE

We are going to look at some very practical steps to Satan-proofing our families, with a lot of emphasis on the power of the Holy Spirit. When you become a bona fide Satan-proofer, you will need the power of God because what you are actually doing is declaring war on Satan. You're saying, "NO!" to the destructive plans he has concocted to bring division and strife into your family. In order to succeed at stopping the devil, it is imperative that you are moving in the power of the Holy Spirit.

You know if there is any place where we need to be led of the Holy Spirit, it's in the privacy of our own homes. There really is a lot of stress in the home situation. You've heard that old saying, "The boss strikes out at you, you go home and strike out at your spouse, your spouse strikes out at the kids, and the kids strike out at the poor dog!" Even though this sounds humorous, that's basically what happens in many family units.

We may not intentionally want to hurt our family members; nevertheless, we tend to strike out and hurt those who are closest to us. When your family has been Satan-proofed by the presence of the Holy Spirit and your boss gets on your nerves, you won't come home and take it out on your spouse or your children or your dog. The Holy Spirit will help you work out your emotional frustrations before you cause trouble for your family.

A lot of you wives are saying, "Marilyn, you don't know my husband. He is as mean as a snake!" On the other hand, some of you wives have become so critical that you just nag, nag, nag your poor husbands; and they are trying as hard as they can to please you. There are others of you whose children have just about driven you up the wall. So, what do you do? You pray (without letting anyone else hear you) in the Holy Spirit, and God will help you to respond to your family in love—even when they are being very unloving toward you.

There is a lot of tension between parents and children. You'll find that your family life will be a lot less stressful if you Satan-proof your relationships with your children by allowing the Holy Spirit to lead you in parenting.

COMMAND YOUR CHILDREN TO SERVE GOD

One of the first things the Holy Spirit will lead you to do concerning your children is to raise them to serve God. Do you remember what God said about Abraham?

. . . he will command his children and his household after him . . . (Genesis 18:19).

God was saying that Abraham would raise his children to serve the Lord. God must have had a lot of confidence in Abraham because these words were spoken before Abraham and Sarah's child was even born. That's quite a compliment; certainly, the best one Abraham ever received. What about your household? What does God say about your parenting techniques? Does He say that you are raising your children up to serve Him?

Maybe you raised your children according to God's Word, but they still went the way of the world and fell into a destructive lifestyle. I understand how you feel; my son got involved in drugs. But I raised him to serve the Lord, and I refused to measure the truth of God's Word according to my son's lifestyle. I know that my son, Michael's, life is going to line up with what God says about him. The Bible says it, and I believe it with all my heart.

Parents are supposed to plant the seed of God's Word into the hearts of their children. We teach them the Bible and keep them exposed to a godly lifestyle. But as far as serving the Lord is concerned, that only happens when their hearts have been changed, and that involves a work of the Holy Spirit.

After Abraham had commanded his children to serve God, the Bible says they kept the way of God:

. . . they shall keep the way of the LORD, to do justice and judgment; that the LORD may bring upon Abraham that which he hath spoken of him (Genesis 18:19).

Why did they continue to serve God? Because Abraham had planted God's Word into their hearts, and the Spirit of the Lord caused them to obey God after they had grown up. You may not know it, but you can't force your children to obey God, especially when they are out of your sight. Obedience to God comes out of the heart. So even though Abraham's children may have started out obeying God simply because it was a household rule, after they grew up and developed a personal relationship with God for themselves, they obeyed God because they loved Him.

The Holy Spirit drew Isaac unto God, and the Holy Spirit will draw your child too:

Train up a child in the way he should go: and when he is old, he will not depart from it (Proverbs 22:6).

One time we got a letter that was so touching from a prisoner who had gotten hold of my book, A *Cry for Miracles*. He said he was a Vietnam war veteran and had been experiencing terrible conflict because he had killed people during the war. As a child he had been taught in Sunday School that it was wrong to kill. After the war, his wife and daughter were drowned in a boating accident. This was so tragic. His letter said he just couldn't take any more, and he simply lost it. He became addicted to drugs, began to write phony prescriptions for codeine, and eventually he ended up in prison: "I just thought there was no hope for me . . . I had been in despair until I read that book. Out of the blackness of where I was, I began to see a little pinpoint of light."

His letter was full of hope, and he intended to go to the prison chaplain and ask for prayer. When I read his letter, I thought, "Wow, somebody way back in his Lutheran background got the Word into him and probably prayed for him." They had Satan-proofed this man as a child; and although he had detoured and suffered through so many terrible experiences, that precious seed had taken root and was now beginning to sprout.

Folks, we are to bring our children up according to God's Word. And, by faith, we must know that God will manifest His will in their lives despite what outward circumstances may look like.

We Christians begin to Satan-proof our children when we dedicate them in church and bring them to Sunday School.

When we do that, I believe that God's supernatural hand comes upon our children. And then God dispatches angels to go before and behind our children not only to protect them but also to cause their lives to stay in line with His Word.

So, what if everything doesn't turn out the way we think it should in our children's lives! There will come a time when God's all-powerful Holy Spirit will draw our children to God through Jesus Christ. I have watched it happen again and again.

I want you to notice that God didn't say Abraham gave his household the option to choose whether or not they would serve God. We can't say to our children, "Well, honey, if you like the Bible then you can read it. But if you don't, well you don't have to read it because I want you to grow up with the freedom to choose." NO! God said Abraham commanded his family to serve the Lord. The word *command* means "to direct with specific authority or prerogative; to order." We are to "direct" or "order" our children in the way of the Lord if we want the blessings of God to follow them.

Abraham commanded his children to serve God, his children commanded their children to serve God, and God honored their obedience and blessed all of them.

What happened with Abraham's children? Well, God told Abraham's son, Isaac, *". . . I will perform the oath which I sware unto Abraham thy father"* (Genesis 26:3).

Abraham's grandson, Jacob, also served God and came under the same covenantal promises:

And the land which I gave Abraham and Isaac, to thee I will give it, and to thy seed after thee will I give the land (Genesis 35:12).

Wise parents raise their children to line up their lives according to God's Word. When we speak the Word to them, we can be certain that God's Word will not return void (see Isaiah 55:11). Although your children may get out of God's will and get into a sinful lifestyle, God will cultivate the godly seed you have planted. The Holy Spirit will continue to draw them until they turn their lives back toward God.

SPIRITUAL INSTRUCTION

If you want your children to be influenced by the Holy Spirit, it's necessary that you first set a personal example. Look at Joshua. He led the children of Israel into Canaan and they took the Promised Land in 6½ years. Joshua was a power house for God, definitely full of the Holy Spirit:

And the LORD said unto Moses, Take thee Joshua the son of Nun, a man in whom is the spirit, and lay thine hand upon him (Numbers 27:18).

I know Joshua's children were influenced by his spiritual walk with God because at the end of his life he said:

And if it seem evil unto you to serve the LORD, choose you this day whom ye will serve; whether the gods which your fathers served that were on the other side of the flood, or the gods of the Amorites, in whose land ye dwell: but as for me and my house, we will serve the LORD (Joshua 24:15).

Joshua knew his family would continue to serve God even after he died. He had Satan-proofed his family by commanding them according to God's Word, and he had led them as he had been led by the Holy Spirit.

Did you know that the Holy Spirit will instruct you in how you should discipline your children?

I met a woman in Chicago—in fact, she had come to pick me up at the airport when I was there for one of my Bible Encounters. As we were visiting in the car, she told me she was a single parent. When her son became a teenager, he became wild and rebellious. She had been a Christian only a couple of years; and she thought, "Oh, God, what am I going to do with this boy? I don't have a husband to really line him up, and he's going through these difficult years. What shall I do?"

The Holy Spirit said to her, "Every time he disobeys or gets into rebellion, have him write down all the scriptures on disobedience and all the scriptures on obedience." So she took her topical Bible and showed her son where all those scriptures could be found and told him to write them all down in longhand.

Every time the son was disobedient or rebellious, his mother made him write down all those scriptures. He spent hours and hours and wrote pages and pages; but, you know, writing all that scripture absolutely cured him! After a while he didn't get into any more rebellion, and he really got turned on to God's Word. He began to serve the Lord and attended Bible school.

By obeying the specific instructions given to her by the Holy Spirit, this lady Satan-proofed her son and protected him from the devil's disgusting attempts to bury him in a lifestyle of rebellion and disobedience.

The Bible shows that God gave specific instructions on parenting to a couple who lived in Zorah. Manoah and his wife didn't have any children because she was barren (see Judges

13:2–3). One day while the wife was out in the field, an angel appeared to her and said, "You're going to have a baby boy." Of course, she was excited and ran to tell her husband what the angel had said. Manoah listened to what his wife said, but he wanted to hear it straight from the angel's mouth:

Then Manoah intreated the LORD, and said, O my Lord, let the man of God which thou didst send come again unto us, and teach us what we shall do unto the child that shall be born (Judges 13:8).

The angel told them the boy was to be raised a Nazarite, which meant he was never to touch anything dead nor drink wine nor cut his hair. The angel also repeated his earlier instructions for Manoah's wife—while she was pregnant, she couldn't eat anything that came from the vine, including wine and strong drink, nor could she eat any unclean thing.

This boy, of course, was Samson; and the Bible says that the Spirit of the Lord began to move him *"between Zorah and Eshtaol"* (see Judges 13:25). He had a very unusual anointing on him; and, although Samson certainly took a few detours, he eventually accomplished God's purpose for his life and destroyed many of Israel's enemies (see Judges 16:30). But before the Spirit of the Lord came upon Samson, God had already done a work in the hearts of his parents.

It was the same way with Joshua. Remember, he said, *"As for me and my house, we will serve the Lord"* (Joshua 24:15). Where did God begin working first? In Joshua's heart. It's very important for parents to understand that God wants to begin working in your heart first, and then He will work in the hearts of your children.

I want to encourage you here because some of you are feeling like such flops as parents. I know how you feel because I've felt the same way—most of us, at one time or another, probably have felt that way. We've thought, "Oh, God! I'm no good at parenting. I'm not sure you should have given me any children. I don't know which way to turn."

God doesn't mind when you get to the point where you don't know what to do next. Usually, that's when you start looking toward Him and asking for direction. It probably would be a lot easier on everyone if you would make a habit of seeking His instruction in every phase of child rearing. We can be assured that as God answered Manoah's prayer for direction in raising Samson, He also will answer you when you seek His direction for your children.

As I said earlier, this chapter has a strong emphasis on the Holy Spirit operating in our homes. Some of you may be wondering, "Who is the Holy Spirit? Where is the Holy Spirit? How can I be instructed by the Holy Spirit?"

Know ye not that ye are the temple of God, and that the Spirit of God dwelleth in you? (1 Corinthians 3:16).

The Holy Spirit is the third member of the Trinity along with the Father and the Son. The Holy Spirit is God; and if you are a born-again believer, the Holy Spirit lives inside your spirit.

There are many names in the Bible that describe different attributes of God. One of them is *El Shaddai*, which means "The God Who is More Than Enough." Job really got a revelation of El Shaddai because when Job had lost his family, health, and wealth, the God Who was more than enough restored everything to Job in double portion (see Job 42:12). Abraham and

Sarah encountered El Shaddai when The God Who is More Than Enough opened Sarah's barren womb, and she conceived Isaac despite the fact that they were long past the childbearing age (see Genesis 21:1–3).

The Holy Spirit is the Spirit of God Who is more than enough, and He has made Himself available to you. When you don't have the answers for the many, many circumstances that come against your family, just remember the Spirit of the living God is waiting with failproof instructions to direct you through any situation coming your way.

How does He instruct you? Sometimes God will give you visions. I've never had very many visions, probably about three that I can recall; but they were wonderful. Most of the instructions that I've received from the Holy Spirit have come like impressions from deep in my spirit. But sometimes the Holy Spirit will instruct you with a scripture, and your answer will become clearer to you as you meditate on God's Word.

There are many scriptures that exhort believers to allow the Holy Spirit to instruct them. You might be thinking, "Well, I'm just not very spiritual. I haven't read through the entire Bible. I don't pray in tongues two or three hours a day. I don't get very excited, and I don't dance or even clap my hands during worship."

But the Bible doesn't say you have to do all of that to be led by the Holy Spirit; so don't try to build up some kind of case with requirements that are too hard for you to handle. The bottom line is that if you've been born again, you're the temple. If you're the temple, you've got the Holy Spirit. If you've got the Holy Spirit, you've got the Instructor. If you've got the Instructor, He can do the work of El Shaddai in your situation. It's that easy, so don't try and make things difficult for yourself.

Another way the Holy Spirit will instruct you is through *unctions*. An *unction* is "a special endowment, an anointing":

But ye have an unction from the Holy One, and ye know all things (1 John 2:20).

The Holy Spirit has given believers a special anointing to *"know all things."* I know, some days you may not feel so smart; but within you is the potential to know all things. I think that's marvelous, especially on the days when I don't feel too swift. It's comforting to know that no matter how tough a situation we may be facing, the Holy Spirit will teach us how to Satan-proof our families and keep the devil from doing any damage to our households while we are dealing with the crisis.

I was on a plane to Atlanta, and one of the flight attendants (I'll call her Rachel) told me she was born again and Spirit-filled. Rachel was unsure as to whether or not she should continue in her profession because sometimes she was required to serve liquor to the passengers. Then she told me about an incident when a man became drunk and began to act very crudely toward the women on the airplane. Rachel started praying in the Spirit and asked God for a revelation on how to handle this man.

The Holy Spirit directed her to go and sit next to the intoxicated man. While she sat there praying quietly, pretty soon the man's hand was on her leg. Rachel moved his hand and said, "I know you have a wonderful wife at home who is praying for you, and you're just living and acting like a dog! What is wrong with you?"

Well, the man was just stunned; and he asked, "How did you know my wife is a Christian and she prays in tongues?" Rachel continued to blast him, "You're a lecherous, lustful man, and I'm going to cast those evil spirits out of you right now!" She did, and the man was set free; and he gave his life to the Lord right there on that airplane.

There were two things working here that I want you to see. First, what was the man's wife doing? She was Satan-proofing her home by praying in the Spirit. How do you think he ended up on that particular flight? It was the Holy Spirit. And then the Holy Spirit gave Rachel a special anointing to handle this specific situation.

Folks, some of you probably don't agree; but I don't believe we can put God in a box and tell Him how, where, or when to use people. I certainly am not advocating Christians to be involved in a sinful lifestyle. But I know that Satan is gaining hold of one precious soul after another because believers have been content to stay hidden away in comfortable church buildings instead of doing what God intended—subduing the earth!

When Rachel, the flight attendant, mentioned her dilemma about her job again, this time the Holy Spirit gave me an unction. I reminded Rachel of Nehemiah, who was the cup-bearer to Artaxerxes, the king of Persia. The Bible says the cup contained wine (see Nehemiah 2:1). So, if God could use Nehemiah despite the fact that he served liquor, He surely could continue to use Rachel too.

SPIRITUAL ENCOURAGEMENT

Remember in Chapter One how we talked about Satan-proofing our relationships by praying in the Holy Spirit (see Jude 20–21)? Now I want to tell you some very practical things concerning how you treat your family members, so you'll know exactly what happens when you pray in the Holy Spirit.

I believe praying in the Spirit gives us a special anointing to love people who maybe aren't so lovable at that particular time. Let's be honest; it's not easy to keep loving a mate who says all kinds of terrible things which cut you to your heart. It's a fact that no one can hurt you as deeply as your spouse or your children. But if you want to keep the devil out of that relationship, you'll have to pray in the Holy Spirit, and God will build you up in those hurting places. God will help you to keep focused on His wonderful love instead of focusing on the offenses, hurts, wounds, or defeats that the devil will try to intensify in your heart.

Praying in the Holy Spirit will reveal God's image of your children to you. Sometimes, I think we Christians really tend to be very critical of our children—we expect them to be so perfect. Folks, our children need our encouragement more than they need any one thing from us as parents. We need to let our children know they are precious and valuable to God as well as to our family unit. Of course, we are to train our children up in the Word of God; we certainly are to administer proper and consistent correction to them. But we also are to help them to understand that we correct them because we esteem them highly. Do your children know they will be better off because you have corrected them? Are they encouraged—built up or edified—after you have corrected them? Or do they just feel worthless and defeated?

The ratio of encouragement to constructive criticism should be 90 percent encouragement to 10 percent criticism. Take time to check yourself out and make sure you are giving out more encouragement than criticism; and then, make sure that the criticism is always constructive. If you find yourself deficient, begin to increase the amount of time you spend praying in the Holy Spirit. God will give you a revelation of how He sees your children, and He will increase your love for them even while they are being rebellious.

I know raising children is difficult, and it's easy to become critical. It's so easy to lose your patience and become fed up with your children, to give up and decide not to deal with them. But let me warn you, if you don't deal with your children, you can bet the devil will! He just loves to see children who feel neglected, unwanted, or inferior. He has all kinds of bright, glittery enticements to offer them—money, drugs, fast cars, and wrong friendships. There are all kinds of vicious things just waiting to swallow your children up, and they will be lost in a subculture from which there is almost no escape.

But we can keep the devil away from our children by encouraging them, and we can receive a special anointing to do this from God when we pray in the Holy Spirit.

Let's talk about knowledge:

. . . *we know that we all have knowledge. Knowledge puffeth up, but charity edifieth* (1 Corinthians 8:1).

We all can know how to treat people. There are thousands of

how-to books and articles available that will give you step-by-step directions to develop a fulfilling relationship with your spouse and children. But it is apparent that this type of knowledge is not working because the failure-of-the-family phenomenon continues to sweep through Christian homes. This is because most believers are not Satan-proofing their families by praying in the Holy Spirit. Most of us are not encouraging ourselves in the love of God concerning our families. Instead we only are gathering knowledge, and knowledge without love has thrown believers into a tremendous pride level.

Many Christians have elevated themselves so high in the vast knowledge available on how to construct healthy relationships that they have become very mechanical in their thinking. People in this kind of pride don't enjoy people—they don't enjoy their children, and they certainly don't enjoy their mates. There is no godly love operating here, but only a feeling of having to be the "expert" or always having to know the correct way to do everything. I think, "How boring to be with someone who knows everything all the time." Even if they were right all the time, I wouldn't want to be around them.

I was a pastor's wife for many years. I have heard this complaint so many times. Your relationships will function so much better if you don't try to be the one who knows everything. And if you do have to know everything, be sure that the first thing you know is all about godly love. This is not the emotional feeling that comes over us from time to time, but the real action of loving—the doing of beneficial things for those with whom we come into contact. You'll only discover this kind of love by spending time praying in the Holy Spirit. Then you'll take His instructions and Satan-proof your household by encouraging, building up, and edifying your family members in God's love.

THE HOLY SPIRIT BRINGS LIFE

Another thing you'll need to have in a Satan-proofed home is the life of God operating in your household. Most Christian homes simply have too much death lurking around. Believers need to bring forth the life of God by praying in the Holy Spirit.

You may be asking yourself, "What does she mean about having no death in my house?" But there are many ways that death can come into your home. One way is through the school systems. If your children attend public schools, you need to be aware that their minds are being filled with death. Of course, they are learning theories, principles, and academics which are necessary for them to function in the world. But there is so much other dead thinking being forced into their minds like evolution, materialism, and how to participate in safe sex.

Death also can infiltrate your household through an unsaved mate. Now I don't want any of you to say, "Marilyn said I should get rid of my unsaved mate." I didn't say that; the Bible assures us that one believing mate sanctifies the household. However, if your mate is unsaved, he (she) is spiritually dead; and you need to counteract that spirit of death with the Spirit of Life. That happens when you regularly pray in the Holy Spirit.

There are other things you need to look at, like the type of music your children listen to. What television programs does your family watch? Satan is subtle, and he won't always come in with a loud crash. Sometimes he will slither in quietly like a snake, but he always brings death and destruction.

In contrast, God always has brought life into dead situations through the power of the Holy Spirit. Look at Genesis 1:1–2— before the creation the earth was in such turmoil, confusion, and havoc. The Spirit of God brooded over the earth and turned chaos (confusion) into cosmos (order). When you start praying in tongues, the Holy Spirit will brood over your household; and He will bring forth life and divine order where there may have been death and confusion. When we pray in the Holy Spirit, we bring life into our situations:

It is the spirit that quickeneth; the flesh profiteth nothing: the words that I speak unto you, they are spirit, and they are life (John 6:63).

Try it. Just begin to walk through your house praying in the Spirit. Pray over your couch; over the kitchen chairs. Husbands and wives can pray over the bed together. Pray over each other's clothes, "Lord, let the person who wears these shoes walk in the life of the Holy Spirit."

I pray over my household all the time. While my husband was a pastor, I always prayed over his pillow and over his clothes. When my daughter Sarah was in school, sometimes I would walk into her room and pray over her bed—asking God to give her special wisdom. I also would ask the Holy Spirit to give her life because I know how students like to stay up so late. I believe that God quickened her mind and her body so she could comprehend and learn better during the day.

Praying in the Spirit is like a thirsty man taking a long drink of water. The more you pray in the Spirit, the thirstier you will become; and the thirstier you become, the more you will pray. It's like a circle. And there is something else:

For I will pour water upon him that is thirsty, and floods upon the dry ground: I will pour my spirit upon thy seed, and my blessing upon thine offspring (Isaiah 44:3).

The more you drink of the Holy Spirit, the thirstier you become; and because of your thirst, God will pour His Spirit out on your children. Then they will begin to thirst after the Spirit of the Lord too. There is a connection in the spirit realm between parents and children. So, if you want your children to become spiritual, make sure you are spiritual and spend a lot of time praying in the Holy Spirit.

LIFT UP A STANDARD

In order to Satan-proof our homes, there must be a standard lifted up against the devil. This comes about when believers become involved in intercessory prayer:

For he put on righteousness as a breastplate, and an helmet of salvation upon his head; and he put on the garments of vengeance for clothing, and was clad with zeal as a cloak (Isaiah 59:17).

Wow! That's the armor of God; quite an outfit isn't it? So, you say, "I'm going to Satan-proof my home through intercessory prayer." Okay, when you put on the breastplate of righteousness, you'll begin to be bolder because you'll be walking in God's righteousness and not your own. The helmet of salvation will protect your mind from thoughts the devil would like you to think. Now the devil will still bring destructive thoughts to you. He'll tell you that you are a failure, your spouse doesn't love you, and your children are the pits—but you don't have to dwell on that kind of junk because your mind is protected by the helmet of salvation.

What does all this sound like? It sounds to me as if someone is preparing for battle! These are battle clothes. You say, "But Marilyn, I'm not going to be out on the mission field or in evangelism fighting to further the gospel. I'm just going to be praying in my bedroom for my family." Then your bedroom will become a battlefield. That's where you are going to take your stand and tell the devil that he cannot have your marriage, children, relatives or friends, finances, future—or anything else that pertains to you!

When you put on the garment of vengeance, God says that He will repay the devil when he comes to your door trying to wreak havoc in your home:

According to their deeds, accordingly he will repay, fury to his adversaries, recompense to his enemies . . . When the enemy shall come in like a flood, the Spirit of the LORD shall lift up a standard against him (Isaiah 59:18–19).

The word *standard* here means "something that causes something else to vanish, flit, or flee.'" James 4:7 says, *"Submit yourselves therefore to God. Resist the devil, and he will flee from you."*

Once you have clothed yourself in the armor of God, then YOU, the intercessor, are the standard that God wants to lift up. Through the power of Christ Jesus, God wants you to resist the devil on behalf of your loved ones. And when you have submitted your life and have begun to develop a more intimate relationship with God, the devil will flee from your home when

41

you command it in Jesus' name. God wants you to Satan-proof your family by becoming such a tremendous intercessor that the devil won't want to waste his time by stopping at your house!

CHAPTER THREE

BLESS YOUR HOUSEHOLD

I think it's important to explain to you that Satan-proofing your home is not just a one-shot deal. I say this because some of you will only put into action one of the principles outlined in this book, and you'll think your home is safe. Then when the devil interrupts your life again, you'll say, "Hey, Marilyn, it didn't work!" But it's not that the principles don't work, it's that they all work together.

Satan-proofing your home is a continuous and progressive lifestyle. It's similar to a puzzle. Receiving Christ as your personal Savior is one piece, reading your Bible is another piece, applying the Word of God to your own flesh and to your circumstances is a piece, praying in the Holy Spirit is a piece, and speaking forth God's blessings is yet another piece. If we put all these pieces into their proper place, pretty soon we'll have a clearer picture of the image in which God created us—His image, the original Satan-proofer!

BLESSINGS AND BENEFITS

I have noticed something special about a Satan-proofed home: it just seems to overflow with wonderful blessings from God.

Did you know that God began to bless people immediately after He created us:

So God created man in his own image, in the image of God created he him; male and female created he them. And God blessed them . . . (Genesis 1:27–28).

The Hebrew word used here for *blessed* means "to kneel." God put Adam and Eve in a kneeling posture—a position of worship. Why? So, He could begin to prosper them with children and give them control over the earth. Of course, we know they got out of the worshipping-God posture and into the worshipping-their-own-desires posture. They blew it big time, not only for themselves but for everyone else as well.

So, we know that it's God's desire to bless His people. I don't mean to say that God is like Santa Claus and gives us gifts like good health, finances, or peace in our homes. These are not gifts, they are benefits that we receive when we keep ourselves in an attitude of worship—they are the results of living a blessed life.

When we begin to apply blessings to our loved ones, we really are saying, "God, put my loved ones in a posture of worship so they can receive the benefits that accompany being in an intimate relationship with You." Isn't that what you really want for your family? Of course, it is. So, when you think about Satan-proofing your home, remember that you need to speak abundant blessings upon your loved ones. Also, remember that you must be living in an attitude of worship to speak blessings. Folks, we just cannot live a sinful lifestyle and expect to remain consecrated in the authority of God. It just doesn't work that way. In order to bless others, we must first be blessed ourselves.

Basically, there are five promises implied in the word *bless*: to benefit, to make whole, to prosper, to make healthy, and to make wealthy. When you speak God's blessing, you are reminding God of His promises. You're saying, "Father, I remind you of Your promises to Your covenant children: to benefit us, to make us whole, to prosper us, and to make us healthy and wealthy."

If you want a Satan-proofed home, then begin to bless your loved ones. The act of blessing is not to be taken lightly, because when we believers mix faith with blessings, we cause God to move on His promises. So whatever circumstance you may be facing, begin to bless the people involved.

There are four areas where God wants His blessings to overflow in the lives of His people: in our circumstances, toward our enemies, toward the Lord, and in our homes.

Wouldn't you like to see God's blessings manifested in all of your circumstances? How about at your workplace? Some of you are experiencing difficulty because your boss favors another employee over you. You have become offended, and you want to jump up and quit. But have you considered that God may want you to stay there to be a conduit for Him to pour out blessings upon those people? Hang in there, and thank God for the job. Begin to bless your boss as well as the other employee. God will bless everyone involved and move on your behalf as well.

Another area where God wants to manifest His wonderful benefits is toward your enemies. You say, "Marilyn, that's where I blow it; I simply cannot bless my enemies."

All right, let's take a closer look at our enemies. We know that our real enemy is the devil. But in terms of people, let's define our enemies as people who either knowingly or unknowingly allow themselves to be used by the devil for the purpose of harming us.

I believe most Christians probably would agree that murderers, robbers, rapists, and the like are our enemies—certainly these people are dangerous. Yet, many of you may have been injured by parents who have neglected or abused you. Some of you have mates who are thoughtless and cruel, or perhaps your mate has deserted you. Others of you have best friends who have begun repeating your deepest secrets! And still others of you may have been manipulated or hurt by another Christian.

There are two things that I want you to see in all these situations: someone has been injured, and someone has been used as a tool by the devil. Certainly, I am not making light of the personal suffering that you may have experienced at the hands of another person, but isn't the person who injured you really just a victim too? I believe Satan uses people against each other to carry out his diabolical schemes to steal, to kill, and to destroy God's people (see John 10:10).

Think about it the next time someone comes against you, and remember that a Satan-proofer can bless his or her enemies. Is it easy? NO! But it can be done by a believer who lives in an attitude of worship, by someone who wants to see God's loving benefits manifested more fully in people's lives:

But I say unto you, Love your enemies, bless them that curse you, do good to them that hate you, and pray for them which despitefully use you, and persecute you (Matthew 5:44).

God also wants to bless us in our relationship with Him:

Bless the LORD, O my soul: and all that is within me, bless his holy name. . . . Who forgiveth all thine iniquities; who healeth all thy diseases (Psalm 103:1–3).

God is blessed by our obedience and praise. He is blessed by our worship. And when we bless God, we create an environment in which the blessings of God can flourish in our lives.

Another area where God wants us to be blessed is in our homes. Given the choice, most of us would like to see God's benefits flow into the lives of our loved ones first. You can bless your children all through the day (God's Word is not bound by time or distance). Speak each child's name and say, "God bless you in your school work." Bless your children especially after they have been disciplined. Go to your child and say, "You have been misbehaving, but I love you; and I am asking God to bless you." I believe that when you mix your faith with the blessing, you'll see an improvement in your child's behavior, attitude, and academic performance.

A woman on my staff has a 15-year-old daughter whose rebellious behavior affected her performance in school. The woman prayed and sought God's wisdom for the situation. Then she began to speak God's blessings into her daughter's life.

As the mother became more aware of the need to speak words of encouragement rather than criticism, the daughter's attitude and academic performance began to improve.

We wives who want to Satan-proof our homes need to bless our husbands—even when they're grumpy or mean.

If he hurts you with unkind words or actions, resist the urge to talk back or pout; instead, pray (to yourself) and speak God's blessings upon him. It's not easy; and some of you may be thinking, "Marilyn, I can't bless my husband. I'd rather strangle him!" Nevertheless, you must bless him—even if you have to say, "God, I'm angry with my husband right now; but by faith I ask You to bless him."

THE PRIESTHOOD AND BLESSINGS

Now let's look at what actually happens when we speak God's blessings. The Bible says that God instructed the priests to bless the children of Israel:

And the LORD spake unto Moses, saying, Speak unto Aaron and unto his sons, saying, On this wise ye shall bless the children of Israel . . . (Numbers 6:22–23).

What happened when the Israelites were blessed?

And Moses and Aaron went into the tabernacle of the congregation, and came out, and blessed the people: and the glory of the LORD appeared unto all the people (Leviticus 9:23).

When the priests blessed the people, God's glory appeared—blessings bring forth a manifestation of the glory of God. You think, "That was fine for ancient Israel, but where are the modern-day priests?" The Bible says that believers are kings and priests:

And from Jesus Christ . . . Unto him that loved us, and washed us from our sins in his own blood, And hath made us kings and priests unto God and his Father . . . (Revelation 1:5–6).

Do you want to see God's glory manifested in your family, your place of employment, your church, the nation, and the world? Then you must take the authority given to you by Christ

Jesus. You must begin to function as a priest to the people with whom you have contact, and start speaking God's blessings into their lives.

I pray and speak God's blessings over my family, ministry and partners, the United States, and the world. Folks, if we want to see God manifest His glory, then we have to stop whining about how bad things are, take our priestly position, and begin to Satan-proof this world!

The Bible clearly tells us the major duties of priests:

At that time the LORD separated the tribe of Levi, to bear the ark of the covenant of the LORD, to stand before the LORD to minister unto him, and to bless in his name, unto this day (Deuteronomy 10:8).

What was so important about the Ark of the Covenant? It contained the Ten Commandments (the way), the golden pot of manna (the truth), and Aaron's rod that budded (the life). The Way, the Truth, and the Life—Who is that? Of course, it's Jesus! The Old Testament priests carried the Ark and those things inside were pictures of the real thing—Jesus!

The Bible also says the priests ministered to God. That means they lived their lives in an attitude of worship. They absolutely could not be in God's presence without being consecrated. And then they blessed people in His name.

What does God want believers—priests—to do today? He wants us to take the love and authority of Jesus to the world. God wants us to live in an attitude of worship, and then He wants us to bless people in the name of Jesus.

One of the many benefits that God wants His people to receive is forgiveness. In order for the Israelites to receive forgiveness for their sins, the Old Testament priests had to offer blood sacrifices. I would have thought, "What a pain to have to kill an animal every time we blow it." I am so glad that we have the New Covenant, which was established through the shed blood of Jesus Christ. We don't have to make any more sacrifices, because one drop of Christ's sinless blood took care of all the sins in the world.

And there's something else about blessings: In Deuteronomy 33:1 we see that Moses blessed the children of Israel before his death. Moses went on to prophesy over all the tribes of Israel. The word *bless* also means "to pronounce good things." What was Moses doing? He was pronouncing good things upon the Israelites.

What about you fathers? Do you pronounce good things upon your children? Do you declare that they are going to do well in school and in their relationships? Do you declare them to be winners in everything that they encounter? If you want to stop the devil from luring your kids away, then you need to begin to bless them. Don't forget, a child who feels that he or she is a worthless loser is vulnerable to Satan's deceptions.

BLESS YOUR CIRCUMSTANCES

Have you ever known someone whose life and circumstances obviously were being flooded with God's glory—but they didn't even know it? A man named Balak, the king of Moab, experienced this very thing.

The Bible tells us how Balak had become very nervous

because the Israelites were passing through Moab on their way to the Promised Land. When Balak heard that they were camped in Moab, he became terrified. He had heard about how the Israelites had killed two Amorite kings, Sihon and Og, and had taken a huge land grant (see Numbers 21:33–35; 22:2–3).

Picture the Israelites—they were ex-slaves who had been in bondage for over 400 years, and they were totally untrained in warfare. Yet they had succeeded in conquering a land that no one else had been able to conquer. It was obvious to everyone that they had supernatural help from God. People were saying, "Did you hear what happened? Those Israelites got all that land when they overcame Sihon and Og. They did it because they worship some kind of God Who blesses them!"

This was also frightening to the Perizzites, the Hivites, and all the rest of those "-ites." Everyone panicked when they heard that the Israelites were coming. After all, Israel had a mighty God Who had parted the Red Sea and had killed all those Egyptians—including Pharaoh! Then Israel's God had helped them kill Sihon and Og—two more kings.

So, when Balak heard the Israelites were in his country, he naturally wondered, "Am I going to die next?" Poor Balak didn't realize that he and his people were blessed because God had commanded the Israelites not to harm them. Why? Because the Moabites were descendants of Abraham's nephew Lot, which made them shirttail relatives of the Israelites, who were direct descendants of Abraham.

Remember when Lot and his two daughters escaped the judgment on Sodom and went to live in a cave in the mountains (see Genesis 19:30–37)? Well, Lot's daughters got him drunk and committed incest with him—yuk, yuk! The oldest daughter named her son Moab, and he became the father of the Moabites.

Despite the Moabites' bad beginning, God had blessed them and had told the Israelites not to harm them. But since Balak didn't know God and he didn't know that the Israelites wouldn't harm the Moabites, he hired the prophet Balaam to curse Israel. Balaam tried and tried to curse the Israelites. He even climbed two different mountains and tried to curse them, but every time he opened his mouth, only blessings came forth. Finally, he said:

Behold, I have received commandment to bless: and he hath blessed; and I cannot reverse it (Numbers 23:20).

Balaam was saying, "I cannot curse these people because they have God's blessings upon them—what God has blessed, no one can curse." What a startling revelation! And, folks, the same thing is true today.

When you begin to Satan-proof your relationships and circumstances by speaking forth the blessings from God, you can believe that no devilish curse can come against them!

Let me show you something about how marital problems and problems with our children are affected by the words we speak. You say, "Christians do not speak curses upon people." But what about the hateful, negative things we say to each other?

What happens when some of you husbands come in from work? You look at your wives and say, "Why do you wear that old thing? You are so fat; when are you going to go on a diet!" Or sometimes you wives say to your husbands, "You have bad breath and body odor—go brush your teeth and take a bath!"

Your poor children—how do you talk to them? Some of you parents say anything, "You'll never amount to anything! Clean up that nasty room; you act just like a pig in a pigpen!"

Are we blessing or are we cursing? If you want the devil to steal your marriage, just continue talking to each other in a negative manner. As far as your children are concerned, I already told you that the devil is on the prowl for children with poor self-esteem; and where do you think your child's self-esteem is developed? In the home, of course.

I know of a young couple who were having some marital problems. One holiday, the wife gave her husband an ultimatum that he would either do things her way, or pack his things and get out!

The husband quickly recognized that the devil was trying to destroy his marriage. So instead of becoming angry, this young believer got out his blessed oil and began to anoint their property including the doors, windows, dresser drawers, and driveway. The husband began to speak blessings on his wife and into their marriage. The couple is together today, and their marriage continues to grow in the Lord.

This young man had a choice, didn't he? He could have just thrown the doors to his marriage wide open and let Satan rob him blind. But instead, he Satan-proofed his household, and spoke blessings upon his circumstances:

Blessings are upon the head of the just: but violence covereth the mouth of the wicked (Proverbs 10:6).

Let me tell you about someone else who blessed his circumstances:

And Esau hated Jacob because of the blessing wherewith his father blessed him: and Esau said in his heart, The days of mourning for my father are at hand; then will I slay my brother Jacob (Genesis 27:41).

I would say that one brother hating another enough to want to kill him is a pretty serious situation, wouldn't you? Why did Esau hate Jacob? Because Jacob had received the firstborn blessing from their father Isaac. As the oldest son, Esau was supposed to inherit the blessing, but he had become careless about spiritual things and had sold his birthright to Jacob for a bowl of stew. However, Esau was not the only one in the wrong; Jacob used a lot of trickery to get the blessing. Esau got so mad at Jacob that he threatened to kill him, but he never did. Why? God's blessings were upon Jacob, and what God had blessed could not be cursed.

When Rebekah found out that her son Esau wanted to kill his brother, she sent Jacob to live with her brother Laban (see Genesis 27:43). Before Jacob left, his father Isaac blessed him again (see Genesis 28:1–4). The Bible tells us that Jacob certainly prospered during the 14 years that he lived in Haran with his uncle Laban. Jacob married two of Laban's daughters, Leah and Rachel, and fathered 12 sons. Jacob also became wealthy:

And the man increased exceedingly, and had much cattle, and maidservants, and menservants, and camels, and asses (Genesis 30:43).

Eventually Jacob returned from Haran to Canaan, and it's interesting to see how he treated Esau. Jacob knew that he could not avoid meeting Esau—I don't think Jacob was looking forward to seeing his brother at all. He knew that he had taken unfair advantage of his brother and that Esau had good reason to be upset.

So, Jacob had an all-night prayer meeting, and God really dealt with him about his own attitude. When Jacob finally did encounter Esau, he didn't reopen the old wound. Instead, Jacob blessed Esau with gifts and allowed God to defuse that potentially explosive situation.

Folks, there is a simple truth working here that we need to get hold of: speaking God's blessings over our circumstances will bring forth God's benefits, and speaking curses over our circumstances will bring forth death.

There was another man who really understood the importance of speaking forth blessings—David:

Then David returned to bless his household. And Michal the daughter of Saul came out to meet David . . . (2 Samuel 6:20).

David had returned from Kiriath-Jearim where he had gone to bring the Ark of the Covenant to his home in Jerusalem. This was a blessed occasion, and there was a tremendous praise and worship service going on—David was leaping and dancing before God with all his might. He went to bless his household, and his wife Michal came out to meet him. Did she graciously receive God's blessings spoken by her husband?

. . . *How glorious was the king of Israel to day, who uncovered himself to day in the eyes of the handmaids of his servants, as one of the vain fellows shamelessly uncovereth himself!* (2 Samuel 6:20).

Michal could have added her blessings to this already glorious occasion, but she did not. Michal did not receive God's blessing through her husband, and she did not bless David back. Rather,

Michal spoke negatively to her husband and dishonored him.

What about your life? Are their times when your spouse or children are in a great mood, and they rush in to share their joy with you—only to have you snap at them or bite off their heads with negative words?

That's what Michal did, and her negative words were a curse. Michal never was able to have children, and she reaped curses for the rest of her life (see 2 Samuel 6:23). On the other hand, from David's descendants came Jesus—David's blessings are eternal.

I believe that some of you wives might feel sorry for Michal and say, "Well, she didn't like the way David was acting, dancing out in the street. She had a right to speak negatively." But let me share with you a woman's testimony of how negative words could have ended her 20-year marriage.

Carol had been standing in faith for her husband and son who were members of a cult. Carol, herself, had been delivered from the cult just months before. Now Carol could have become really negative with her husband—after all she had been born again, she had the truth. She could have been very harsh and said, "Get out of there; because if you don't, you're going to hell!"

But negative words could have ended her marriage. So, Carol didn't speak negative, critical words; instead she got involved in Bible study and began to bless her marriage. She prayed for her family and began to thank God for her husband. Less than a year later both her husband and son came to the Lord and were Spirit-filled.

When we Satan-proof our circumstances by speaking forth God's blessings, we reap blessings. But speaking forth negative words only brings a curse.

God wants us to bless each other's circumstances too like Joshua blessed Caleb:

And Joshua blessed him, and gave unto Caleb the son of Jephunneh Hebron for an inheritance (Joshua 14:13).

Joshua had led the Israelites into the Promised Land, and now he was getting the people situated into the areas where they were supposed to settle. Caleb had said, "Joshua, I want that piece of land that I claimed when we first came to Canaan as spies." So Joshua blessed Caleb and gave him the land he desired.

When we follow Caleb's life, we see that he was one of the most blessed men of God. And Caleb blessed his daughter Achsah even after she married and left his care. She ended up marrying a Spirit-filled man named Othniel, who later became the first judge in Israel.

In our day, it's relatively easy for young girls to find Spirit-filled men to marry. But during those times, it was very unusual for people to become Spirit-filled. So Achsah's marriage really was blessed, and Caleb had a lot to do with her circumstances.

I think Caleb was a very wise father. Sadly, many parents today want to get their children out of their homes quickly; and therefore, they aren't too concerned with whom their children become involved. But Caleb made the announcement that whoever wanted to marry Achsah would first have to kill some giants and take their land (see Joshua 15:16). This may have seemed to be an impossible challenge, but during that time there were giants living in the land. Caleb had killed a few of them, and he wanted to be sure that his daughter's husband could protect her from every type of enemy.

By requiring that his son-in-law be a giant killer, Caleb assured Achsah that her husband would not be lazy—lazy men do not fight giants. Also, she would be assured that her husband would be absolutely wild about her—only the man who sincerely loved her would be willing to risk his life to marry her.

Achsah probably wished her father hadn't issued that challenge. I am certain that her chances of finding a husband who would kill a giant looked very slim. But then *Othniel*, whose name means "force of God," showed up; and he certainly lived up to his name.

You see, Caleb was blessed by God and by men. He wisely blessed the future circumstances of Achsah's life by making it impossible for just anyone to marry her. I cannot emphasize this enough; parents need to bless their children—in every way. We also need to bless our children's future mates, before they ever meet.

The last example I want to give you about blessing each other's circumstances is Ruth, a Moabitess. Remember the Moabites were cursed because of the incestuous relationship between Lot and his daughter, and sexual sin carries a terrible curse (see Deuteronomy 27:20–23).

Ruth also had been brought up in idolatry. The Moabites worshiped an idol called *Chemosh*, which means "a dunghill deity." Idolatry also carries a curse—so Ruth was in double trouble! But both of those curses were absolutely reversed when Ruth turned to God. When she renounced Chemosh, the curses were broken totally and tremendous blessings came upon Ruth.

After Ruth's husband died, she decided to return to Bethlehem with Naomi instead of staying in Moab with her own family. She said to Naomi:

. . . Intreat me not to leave thee, or to return from following after thee: for whither thou goest, I will go; and where thou lodgest, I will lodge: thy people shall be my people, and thy God my God (Ruth 1:16).

When they arrived in Bethlehem, Ruth went to work gleaning in the field of Naomi's wealthy relative Boaz. She followed Naomi's advice, and very soon Boaz wanted to marry Ruth. He went to the elders of the city and went through the tedious legal procedures involved with marrying Ruth (see Ruth 4). There were a lot of legalities that had to be worked out regarding property and children; but Boaz finally got everything straightened out, and he and Ruth were married.

Look at the blessings that the elders spoke into Boaz and Ruth's marriage:

. . . The LORD make the woman that is come into thine house like Rachel and like Leah, which two did build the house of Israel . . . And let thy house be like the house of Pharez whom Tamar bare unto Judah, of the seed which the LORD shall give thee of this young woman (Ruth 4:11–12).

This ceremony was not only about a man taking a wife. More importantly, the elders also were blessing the circumstances of Boaz and Ruth's life together. The elders prayed for Ruth to be like Rachel and Leah, Jacob's wives who had borne the children who became the heads of the twelve tribes of Israel. The elders also prayed for Ruth to be like Judah's daughter-in-law, Tamar, who had borne twin sons, Pharez and Zarah (see Genesis 38:11–30). The children of these three women were blessed, and the elders were speaking the same blessings upon Ruth. But could Ruth's offspring be such a blessing? After all Rachel, Leah, and Tamar were Israelites while Ruth was a Moabitess.

You see, the Israelites knew the prophecy recorded in Genesis 3:15:

And I will put enmity between thee and the woman, and between thy seed and her seed; it shall bruise thy head, and thou shalt bruise his heel.

This is a Messianic prophecy, and all the Israelite women wanted to bring forth that seed. However, the Messiah would come only through the lineage of Judah:

The sceptre shall not depart from Judah, nor a lawgiver from between his feet, until Shiloh come; and unto him shall the gathering of the people be (Genesis 49:10).

The Bible records five women in the genealogy of Jesus Christ, and Ruth is among these women (see Matthew 1:5). Do you wonder how she got there? Well, Boaz was from the tribe of Judah, and he and Ruth had a son named Obed. Obed's son was Jesse, and Jesse was the father of David. Ruth was David's great-grandmother; so, she wound up in the genealogy of Jesus Christ!

God's blessings absolutely are powerful, and I pray that you will become a Satan-proofer and begin to function as a priest to the people closest to you. As you speak forth God's wonderful blessings, people will come into an attitude of worship and begin to walk in the tremendous benefits that accompany the manifestation of God's glory!

CHAPTER FOUR

COMING OUT OF THE CLOSET

Have you noticed lately that all kinds of people are coming ''out of the closet," and they are demanding that the whole world acknowledge who they are and exactly what they are doing! Regardless of the lifestyle in which they may be involved, these people want to be noticed—they want their lifestyles to be accepted as normal.

God wants His people to set a strong example for what is the normal lifestyle—we Christians should be the ones who are most noticed. I travel all over the world, and I have become concerned that many Christians seem to have become confused about what is involved in living a truly Christian lifestyle.

Many of us are quick to say that we are following Christ's example—but do you know that wherever Jesus went, He caused a stir? His lifestyle included preaching the gospel, healing the sick, feeding the poor, and getting people delivered from the devil. Folks, you can't lead that kind of lifestyle without stirring up something!

You say, "Well, that refers to people in leadership positions. I'm not called to go out and minister to large crowds of people." Maybe you're not, but aren't we Christians supposed to minister to the people with whom we come in contact—like family, friends, co-workers, hairdressers, or gas station attendants? Let me ask you, does the cashier at your favorite grocery store know you are a Christian? What about your neighbors? Or your doctor? Or even your in-laws?

Is the fact that you have been born again and baptized in the power of the Holy Spirit making a difference in anyone's life other than your own? If not, then you need to come out of the closet so that Jesus can use you to do His Father's work here on earth.

When I say, "come out of the closet," I am referring to coming out of the complacent mindset held by so many believers today. The word *complacent* means "to be pleased with oneself or one's situation often without awareness of some potential danger." Many of us are self-satisfied because we attend church, we don't drink, smoke, or commit adultery—we think we are imitating Christ. But living a clean lifestyle alone does not reflect Christ. Of course, Jesus lived a clean life; however, He also preached the gospel, healed the sick, fed the hungry, and delivered people from the clutches of Satan. Ask yourself, "Am I really imitating Christ, or have I become complacent in a lifestyle that has little effect on anyone other than myself?"

GOD + YOU = A MAJORITY

Satan-proofers are people who know they *"can do all things through Christ Who strengthens"* them (see Philippians 4:13). They are believers who have come out of the closet and have taken charge of their circumstances. Satan-proofers bring about change when, by faith, they step out of the comfort zone of familiarity and begin to apply God's Word to the world around them—beginning first in their own lives. Applying God's Word to your environment will bring a change—maybe not always a pleasant change—but always a necessary change. These changes will bring our environment into order according to Biblical principles.

Change isn't easy because many Christians would rather lean on someone than be leaned on. They would rather be prayed for than to pray for someone else. It's easier for some of us to blend into the background like chameleons rather than to do what God has called all believers to do—subdue the earth.

Remember *to subdue* means "to tread down, to conquer, to bring into bondage." You may be thinking, "The earth is so big, and there are so many people with so many situations. How does God expect us to have an effect on so many different lives?" It's easy; you do it one person at a time. You begin by extending God's love to your family and friends. Pretty soon, you'll be praying and blessing your co-workers, hairdresser, gas station attendant—and don't forget the cashier at the grocery store.

When every believer begins to Satan-proof the small part of the earth over which he or she has influence, then the whole earth will be subdued! Won't that be marvelous? But it won't happen until believers courageously come out of the closet, take a stand, and Satan-proof God's beautiful earth.

As you begin to emerge from the closet, don't be discouraged when the devil starts telling you that you can't win, or that you are all alone. DON'T LISTEN! The devil is a liar! The Bible says that Jesus is always with you, and that you *can do all things through Christ which strengthens you* (see Matthew

28:20; Philippians 4:13). You can succeed in Satan-proofing your environment because Jesus is with you and God plus you always equals the majority.

HIDING YOUR CHRISTIAN IDENTITY

Let's look at the life of a young woman named Esther who took charge of her circumstances and literally changed the world! Her situation was very serious, and her actions could have cost her life; but Esther came out of the closet and saved the people of Israel.

The events recorded in the book of Esther took place while the Israelites were being held in Babylonian captivity. The story begins when Persia's King Ahasuerus (also referred to as King Xerxes) threw a party that lasted six months—it was a very extravagant occasion. Ahasuerus spared no expense wining and dining the leaders of the 127 provinces of the Persian Empire. And since it was not customary for men and women to feast together, Queen Vashti was busily entertaining the wives of these leaders in another part of the palace.

Jewish tradition says that Ahasuerus apparently became overcome by the wine because he demanded his wife Vashti to come in naked and display herself to his guests! You know, every time I read this I say to myself, "What a jerk!" I'm not involved in the women's liberation movement, but I certainly believe Vashti acted in good taste when she refused her husband's demands. However, Vashti's refusal presented quite a problem for Ahasuerus. His seven counselors immediately began to warn him that he had better do something about his rebellious wife before all the women in the empire followed Vashti's example and rebelled against their husbands. One counselor, Memucan, went so far as to advise the king to divorce Vashti and choose another queen more befitting the position (see Esther 1:19). Even though Ahasuerus may have loved Vashti, to save face, he divorced her. Ahasuerus may have been king over the most powerful empire of that day, but he allowed himself to lose his wife because of his own pride and the unwise counsel of his advisors.

You're probably thinking, "I would never be that stupid!" Hopefully not, but what about the times when you have blown it with your mate? Did you quickly apologize and make up? Or did you let your little mistake escalate into a full-blown incident? Did you call a friend for advice? Did your friend give you godly advice that would reconcile you with your mate? Or did you call someone you knew would sympathize and take sides with you?

I know a woman who had been very unhappily married. Her husband abused her physically, drank a great deal, and was neither loving nor understanding. Soon she became involved with another man. It was a very bad situation, and there was no question of her guilt.

We prayed with this woman and we gave her godly counsel to humble herself before the Lord as well as before her husband. She broke off her relationship with the other man, and then she humbled herself before her husband.

She said, "I have done wrong, and I do not deserve to be your wife." In no way did the woman blame her husband for anything! She humbled herself.

However, her husband would not accept her apology, and

he divorced her. But one year later God had done a work in the husband's life. My husband had the privilege of remarrying them, and they are married to this day! We counseled this wife according to God's Word—to submit and humble herself before her husband (see 1 Peter 3:1). I'm sure it wasn't easy, but she received and acted upon our godly counsel and God mercifully intervened and saved her marriage.

The devil does not care how he gets into your relationships—his only goal is to infiltrate and cause trouble. Satan doesn't have any problem using your pride to destroy your relationships. If you are going to Satan-proof your home, it's important that you never allow pride to hinder you from reconciling with your loved ones. Come out of the closet. Come out of your comfort zone. Don't wait for things to blow over; bring your circumstances in line with the Word of God!

Even though King Ahasuerus certainly did everything wrong concerning the situation with Queen Vashti, God did get the glory out of the next queen of Persia. After Ahasuerus and Vashti's divorce, the king's servants decided to have a beauty contest to choose the next queen:

Then said the king's servants that ministered unto him, Let there be fair young virgins sought for the king (Esther 2:2).

They went to all 127 provinces and brought back the most gorgeous women in the empire. Among these women was a lovely, young Jewish girl named *Hadassah*, which means "myrtle tree." Of course, no one knew she was Jewish because she was known by the name *Esther*, which means "a star." Esther's parents were dead, and she lived with her cousin Mordecai (see Esther 2:7).

With Mordecai's help Esther had been living among the Persian people in the closet with her Jewish heritage carefully hidden.

I can think of occasions when it could be convenient to let our Christian values slide. For instance, consider the single mother who is concerned that the posters on her teenage son's bedroom walls are somewhat seductive. This mother knows that her son tends to be rebellious and that he gets angry easily. Should this mother insist that her son remove the posters, or should she simply leave well enough alone and thank God that at least the boy is not on drugs or in a street gang?

If this mother wants to Satan-proof her teenager, then she has to enforce godly principles in her home. She cannot leave well enough alone, she has to come out of the closet and create a stir in her son's life.

Let's relate this to Esther, who had not revealed her Jewish heritage but went on to win the beauty contest:

And the maiden pleased him, and she obtained kindness of him; and he speedily gave her her things for purification ... (Esther 2:9).

I wonder how many of you Christian husbands get upset when your wives spend too much time in the beauty parlor? It may take your wife three or four hours; it took Esther a whole year to be prepared to meet the king. Esther soaked in exquisite perfumes and exotic bath oils for one solid year! Sometimes when I would get home from having my hair done, my husband Wally would tease me, "Oh, I guess they couldn't take you today, Marilyn."

But I know Wally appreciated the fact that I took care of myself.

It's sad to say, but many women think the beautification process stops once the wedding is over. However, really that's when it all begins. I know, sometimes it takes more effort than you may want to put forth, but we women have to come out of our closets of complacency and extend that extra effort. I believe taking care of your physical appearance and hygiene is part of Satan-proofing your marriage. Believe me, if you don't care how you look or smell, before long you will put your husband in a vulnerable position from which he could be tempted by the devil to stray from your marriage.

So, Esther spent one year preparing to go before the king and she had favor with everyone who looked upon her. Do you know that God can give you favor with unsaved people?

I want to encourage young people; you may think that nobody will like you because you are a Christian. But if you'll be true to God, He will give you favor and make you the pivotal point of your school. God will use you as a vessel to bless other people. First, you will have to come out of the closet and let people know that you love Jesus, then God will bless you.

Four years after the big 180-day feast where Vashti had rebelled, Esther finally was taken before Ahasuerus, and she really must have been a knockout:

And the king loved Esther above all the women, and she obtained grace and favour in his sight more than all the virgins; so that he set the royal crown upon her head, and made her queen instead of Vashti (Esther 2:17).

Ahasuerus married Esther, and this young, Jewish girl became his queen (see Esther 2:17). Sometimes when I read this book, I wonder about Mordecai. After all, he was encouraging Esther to remain in the closet, hiding the fact that she was one of

God's chosen people. Even after Esther and Ahasuerus married, Mordecai told her to remain hidden (see Esther 2:20). Little did they know that they were God's providence for a big crisis which was just over the horizon.

STARS SHINING IN THE DARKNESS

I really enjoy studying about the providence of God. It's wonderful to know that we believers are still God's provision for the people in the world despite the fact that we sometimes fail Him. There are so many times when we allow the pressures of life to hinder us from carrying God's light into a situation.

Years ago, one of our faithful volunteers decided she would surprise me by painting one of the Sunday school rooms at our church. She picked out the color, and she and her son painted the room—they wanted to surprise me. When my husband took me into the room, I looked at the walls and said, "Oh, what a terrible color!" I didn't know the woman and her son were hiding in the closet. Of course, this precious lady was devastated! She ran out of the church, and I ran behind her apologizing and asking her to forgive me. When she got into her car, I stuck my head in the window to tell her how sorry I was; but she just rolled up the window and drove off.

Wouldn't you say that as a pastor's wife, I had blown it? You're right, I did. So, I went home and prayed about it, and I believe the Lord quickened Colossians 1:20 in my spirit:

And, having made peace through the blood of his cross, by him to reconcile all things unto himself; by him, I say, whether they be things in earth, or things in heaven.

I repented for my actions, applied the blood of Jesus to this situation, and asked God to reconcile me to this lady. Before the night was over, she called me and said, "Marilyn, I can't be angry with you. My father is ill, and I need you to pray with me."

Let's face it; we just don't do everything right all the time! That's why it is so encouraging to know that even when we blow it, God can still use us like stars to reflect the light of Jesus Christ and to dispel the darkness that is attempting to cover the earth.

Has there ever been a time in your life when you have failed to reflect the light of Christ, perhaps in a witnessing situation? Some of you think that witnessing is the hardest thing in the world to do. You say, "Oh, I'm just too embarrassed to talk to strangers." Others say, "Everyone has to find his own way. I am not going to force my religious beliefs upon anyone."

Do you think this way? Then, you need to come out of the closet if you want to be a Satan-proofer. Maybe you won't witness like the next person does, but believers are witnesses of God's power in the earth. As you continue to spend time praying and developing your relationship with our wonderful heavenly Father, I believe God will help you to understand better what He wants you to do. God will help you to come out of your closet, and He will use you to reflect the love of Christ—whether you think you're doing it right or not.

It's interesting to see how God brought Esther out of her closet and used her to light up a dark situation. God certainly got a lot of mileage out of Esther's position as queen of Persia because her relationship to the king saved the Israelites from certain destruction.

Then something very interesting happened to Mordecai:

. . . while Mordecai sat in the king's gate, two of the king's chamberlains, Bigthan and Teresh, of those which kept the door, were wroth, and sought to lay hands on the king Ahasuerus (Esther 2:21).

Mordecai had overheard these men plotting to assassinate the king! He quickly sent word to Esther; the two would-be assassins were caught and hanged and Ahasuerus' life was saved. Now you would think the king would be grateful to the man who had saved his life, wouldn't you? But the Bible says only that although the incident was written down in the record books, no gratitude was extended to Mordecai for his loyalty. I think the king could have at least invited Mordecai for dinner. Do you sometimes feel that no one notices the good things you do?

I believe that our young people often feel that no one ever notices the good things they do. As parents, we are quick to point out their mistakes, but do we issue out as much praise for their accomplishments? They so often are confronted with peer pressure in school. They are under a level of temptation that we probably never experienced, and they try so hard to stay true to God. Then when it comes time to get a date for the prom, Christian teens often aren't asked. Why? Because holding true to God's principles sometimes makes them very unpopular, and being popular is extremely important to a teenager.

We need to encourage our young people and take notice when they overcome an obstacle, study extra hard for a subject they hate, say "no" to drugs, or refuse to participate in safe-sex. As parents, we must be careful about how we relate to our children. Like it or not, they will follow our example when deciding whether or not to come out of the closet and share their faith with their peers.

REFUSE TO COMPROMISE

About five years after Esther had been crowned queen, the king promoted Haman to the position of Grand Vizier—Ahasuerus' right-hand man (see Esther 3). Haman really was a very proud man who had a burning passion to be exalted above everyone else. Because of his high position in the Persian Empire, Haman was revered, and people bowed down to him—everyone, except Mordecai.

Although the king's servants repeatedly warned Mordecai about not bowing to Haman, Mordecai would not compromise; he held his ground and refused to reverence Haman.

Mordecai was not being rebellious; he was obeying the Jewish teaching which forbade him to bow down and worship a man. Also, I believe Mordecai probably knew that Haman was a descendant of the Amalekites who were ancient enemies of the Israelites and were considered to be cursed (see Deuteronomy 25:19).

At any rate, Mordecai would not bow and Haman was furious! Haman knew that Mordecai was Jewish, and Haman hated the Jews because the Israelites had defeated his ancestors (the Amalekites) in a war under the leadership of Moses. So, Haman not only wanted to get his hands on Mordecai but also to set into action a diabolic plan to destroy all the Jews in the Persian Empire.

Doesn't that sound like something the devil would do? All the Jews had not offended Haman, only Mordecai. We Christians have been known to make mountains out of molehills when we take on an offense. Many times, we allow a tiny, insignificant offense to grow until it gets blown so far out of proportion that it sometimes is difficult to bring things back into perspective.

Have you ever found yourself in that situation? I have. But I have learned that when I deal with people-problems according to the Bible, God lights up that situation and brings it back into line with His Word every time.

In contrast, Haman used treachery and slander to coax King Ahasuerus into signing an order to destroy, kill, and cause to perish all Jews in the 127 provinces of the Persian Empire.

In my opinion, Ahasuerus' leadership qualities absolutely were the pits! First, he let himself become so intoxicated that he demanded that his wife degrade herself in front of a bunch of drunken men. Next, Ahasuerus followed the terrible advice of his counselors to divorce Vashti because she refused to obey him. Then the king chose his new wife, Esther, through a beauty contest. And now we see this so-called great king letting himself be manipulated into signing an irreversible document which literally would create an open season for killing God's people!

The Bible says that after the devilish decree ordering the murder of the Jewish people went out, the king and Haman sat down to have a drink. But the people of Shushan were perplexed because the Persians had no hatred for the Jewish people. So, for their king to have issued this decree seemed quite out of the ordinary.

I believe that is exactly what the devil does to our circumstances. Many times, when we are experiencing a crisis in our lives, the devil may be influencing the thinking or actions of the people involved. But as Satan-proofers, we have made the choice to come out of our closets and allow the light of God to shine brightly in a potentially dark situation.

Let's look at how Mordecai and Esther came out of the closet of complacency and began to counteract this death sentence pronounced on the Jewish people.

When Mordecai found out what Haman had done, Mordecai tore his clothes and began to cry a loud and bitter cry in the middle of the city. Also, a great cry went up in every province that received the king's decree. The Jewish people began to fast and to cry out. Finally, Esther's attendants told her what had happened. She confirmed it with Mordecai, and Mordecai told Esther that she needed to go to the king and intercede on behalf of the Jewish people.

After all these years of hiding in the closet of complacency, Mordecai told Esther that she would have to "rock the boat" and take a stand for her people. This presented a serious problem because it was not customary for the queen to go and see the king without first being summoned. Esther hadn't been summoned by her husband for a month. If she just barged into the inner court, the king could have killed her (see Esther 4:11). Naturally, Esther was hesitant, but Mordecai told her:

. . . *Think not with thyself that thou shalt escape in the king's house, more than all the Jews* (Esther 4:13).

In other words, Mordecai merely was reminding Esther that if all the Jews were killed, she would be killed too. Perhaps Esther had become so comfortable living a lie that she actually had forgotten that she was Jewish too!

That's not difficult to understand; I believe many Christians have turned from or forgotten that we are Christ's hands extended in the earth. When Christ was physically on earth, He preached the gospel, healed the sick, fed the poor, and delivered people from the devil. God wants believers to do the same, first in our own homes and then in our communities and the world.

Listen, as Esther emerges from her closet:

Go, gather together all the Jews that are present in Shushan, and fast ye for me . . . and if I perish, I perish (Esther 4:16).

After three days Esther dressed up and entered the inner court. There was something special about Esther because when Ahasuerus saw her, he held out his golden scepter indicating that she was to come forward.

You know, there comes a time when God calls each of us to a place of commitment; and we must say, "Even if they all dislike me or if everyone rejects me, I love You Father and I am going to obey You." Esther came out of the closet and made that commitment.

Did you notice, Esther did not just barge into the king's presence; she first prepared herself inwardly. I think this is important in our lives today because whatever we do for God—whether witnessing, laying hands on people, giving out food, or interrelating with people, including our family members—we need to be spiritually in line with God's Word. Along with inward preparation, we also need to be prepared outwardly because the way we present ourselves has a great deal to do with how people respond to us.

Esther invited Ahasuerus and Haman to have dinner with her. I am sure she was a very gracious hostess because the two men accepted a second invitation to join Esther for dinner the next night also.

Haman was absolutely beside himself with excitement. He went home and told his wife, "Oh Zeresh, I am so wonderful. The king thinks so highly of me, and now even his wife Esther wants to have me for dinner. The only thing that bothers me is that Mordecai still refuses to exalt me!" Haman's wife, Zeresh, said, "Well, build a gallows and tomorrow get the king to hang Mordecai; then go to your banquet." Haman pridefully followed his wife's evil counsel.

That very same night King Ahasuerus couldn't sleep, so he decided to read. "Bring me the book that records all the people who have blessed me," he ordered. The king read about the attempt to assassinate him, and he came upon Mordecai's name. He asked his servants:

. . . *What honour and dignity hath been done to Mordecai for this?* . . . (Esther 6:3).

His servants responded that nothing had been done to reward Mordecai. Just then Haman came in to talk with King Ahasuerus about hanging Mordecai. The king asked Haman, "What can I do to honor a man in whom I delight?" Haman had such a tremendous ego that he thought the king was referring to him, so he answered, "Give the man royal clothes worn by the king himself. Let him ride through the city on the king's horse. And tell everyone that the king delights in him."

Haman was shocked when the king said, "That's a great idea. Go out and get Mordecai, and do all those things for him." I am sure that Mordecai was equally shocked when he saw Haman coming with all of that finery. He probably couldn't believe his ears when Haman led him through the city saying:

. . . Thus shall it be done unto the man whom the king delighteth to honour (Esther 6:11).

God has a way of turning a situation around, doesn't He? If we Christians will come out of our closets of complacency and fulfill God's plan for our lives, great blessings will flow in our lives—and through us to others.

Unfortunately, blessings didn't flow into Haman's life. The king's servants took him to Esther's dinner party, and the king probably was on pins and needles wondering what Esther wanted. Finally, she said, "I want my people to be saved, because they have been condemned to death." Ahasuerus said, "What do you mean, your people?" Esther threw back the covers on her life and said, "I am a Jewess."

I love Esther's courage; once she made up her mind, she didn't back down from her commitment. When Haman heard what the queen had said, he knew he was doomed! King Ahasuerus was so upset that he went for a walk in the garden. Haman became so overwrought that he ran over to the queen and fell on the couch where she was reclining. I don't think Haman was trying to rape Esther, but when King Ahasuerus saw them, he sure thought so:

. . . Then said the king, Will he force the queen also before me in the house? . . . (Esther 7:8).

King Ahasuerus had Haman arrested, and they hanged Haman on the same gallows that he had constructed for Mordecai. Then the king gave all Haman's property to Esther. When Esther explained that Mordecai was her cousin, Ahasuerus honored him again and Esther gave Haman's house to Mordecai.

Persian law did not allow a decree to be reversed, so the king wrote another letter granting the Jewish people the right to defend themselves against anyone who would try to kill them. Ahasuerus dispatched this second decree to every province:

The Jews had light, and gladness, and joy, and honour (Esther 8:16).

The Bible says that on the date which had been designated to begin killing the Jewish people:

The Jews gathered themselves together in their cities . . . and no man could withstand them; for the fear of them fell upon all people. (Esther 9:2).

All the Jewish people were saved because two people, Esther and Mordecai, came out of their closets and took their places as God's people.

Likewise, the more you develop your relationship with God, the more your enemies will see Christ in your life. Proverbs 16:7 says:

When a man's ways please the LORD, he maketh even his enemies to be at peace with him.

When you come out of your closet of complacency and begin to show the love and power of God in your life, some of your enemies are going to become Christians—those who once were against you are going to be for you! Why? Because you are a Satan-proofer who is not afraid to let the light of Jesus Christ shine forth brightly in your lifestyle. And as people behold God's love through you, they will be drawn to Jesus; Whose life, death, and resurrection make it possible for all men to receive everlasting life.

CHAPTER FIVE

MARK YOUR HOUSEHOLD

Have you ever known anyone who thought they were hell-bound? There are people who actually think that hell is their destiny! But I want to tell you that hell—the place of eternal torment—is not the destiny of people. Hell was prepared specifically for the devil and his angels (see Matthew 25:41).

Let me clarify the difference between destiny and destine. *Destiny* means "something that is going to happen or has happened to a particular person or thing; lot or fortune; the pre-determined, usually inevitable or irresistible, course of events." However, *destine* means "to set apart for a particular use, purpose; to design or intend; to appoint or ordain beforehand."

The primary point I want you to focus on here is that a *destiny* is usually inevitable or irresistible, while to *destine* is—to set apart—to single out—to mark.

I received a powerful testimony from a man who calls himself the Lone Ranger. He wrote: "I drove an 18-wheeler cross country and did everything under the sun that was sinful, including drugs, alcohol, and hired prostitutes regularly, even though I had a wife and three children at home."

Eventually his wife died, and his children, who hated him,

blamed him for their mother's death. The Lone Ranger stole the truck he was driving, and this 50-year-old trucker ended up in prison.

By his lifestyle, this man certainly may have appeared to have been hell-bound, but I want to tell you that God had marked the Lone Ranger. This man was destined to become born again! His new birth took place while he was in prison: God delivered him from the addictions and gave him a new wife and family. Now he is the New Lone Ranger, and he is a tremendous witness for God's mercy and grace.

GOD HAS MARKED YOUR LOVED ONES

Jesus Christ made it possible for you and me to reach the goal that God had destined us to achieve—eternal life:

For God so loved the world, that he gave his only begotten Son, that whosoever believeth in him should not perish, but have everlasting life (John 3:16).

All people are destined—set apart—for a particular use: to subdue the earth, to be blessed, and to be put in an attitude of worship (see Genesis 1:27–28). God created people in His own image, and we are destined—marked—to bear fruit and to govern the earth. But first, we must renew our minds and be conformed to the image of Christ (see Romans 8:29). The renewing of our minds begins with repentance.

God has marked all people to repent and become born again so they can spend eternity with Him in heaven:

The Lord is not . . . willing that any should perish, but that all should come to repentance (2 Peter 3:9).

The word *repent* means "to change your mind and attitude." God wants people to change their minds and become born again, so we can attain the goal that God has destined (appointed) for all people—to live eternally with Jesus Christ. Isn't that why Jesus lived, died, and was resurrected? Yes, it is. And God decided before the foundation of the world that His precious human creation would be destined to receive eternal life through Christ Jesus.

As Satan-proofers our job is to mark our households for God. We are to single out or to leave an impression upon our loved ones by setting ourselves in agreement with God's will for their lives.

Let me give you an example: For years my husband Wally and I prayed for one of our relatives who was a homosexual. You know, many of our loved ones are caught up in bondage. If someone you love is involved in this terrible perversion, be sure to set yourself in agreement with God's view of the individual sinner rather than how you see the sin.

Please don't think that I am making light of homosexuality. It's a terrible sin, and the Bible says the wages of sin is death (see Romans 6:23). But God loves all people, including homosexuals—not their sin—but the actual person. Homosexuality certainly is a horrendous sin, but it is not an unforgivable sin (see Luke 12:10). Let's begin to pray for our loved ones so they can get on the right track and receive what God has destined for their lives.

Wally and I marked this relative for Jesus. We set ourselves in agreement with God's will for his life. In Jesus' name, we persisted in rebuking Satan and binding the evil spirits that were involved. We regularly prayed for him and kept calling God's attention to his life. We also made an impression in his life by sharing God's Word and by allowing God's wonderful love to shine through us into our relative's life. We never turned our backs on him, and God brought him through. One day this man accepted Christ and was filled with the Spirit. After he was born again he visited different churches and gave a tremendous testimony about God's power to deliver people from sin.

When you become born again; you actually mark your loved ones to receive Christ as Savior too:

. . . *Believe on the Lord Jesus Christ, and thou shalt be saved, and thy house* (Acts 16:31).

When we Christians begin to Satan-proof our relatives, we actually take part in marking them off, singling them out, or calling God's attention to our loved ones. It's easy to do; you can begin now to mark your household by praying, "Father, I so thank You for all my loved ones, and I am marking them off for You. In the mighty name of Jesus, I claim them to be born again, Spirit-filled, and available for You to use in Your kingdom!"

There is something else I want you to see that God has destined for people—the infilling of His Holy Spirit:

...I will pour out of my Spirit upon all flesh: and your sons and your daughters shall prophesy, and your young men shall see visions, and your old men shall dream dreams: And on my servants and on my handmaidens I will pour out in those days of my Spirit; and they shall prophesy (Acts 2:17–18).

What a tremendous time in the history of God's dealings with mankind! God will continue to pour out His Spirit until it has fallen upon all flesh. This means the gift of God's glorious Spirit is available for all our loved ones.

When my daughter Sarah was just a baby, I marked her with Joel 2:28:

And it shall come to pass afterward, that I will pour out my spirit upon all flesh: and your sons and your daughters shall prophesy, your old men shall dream dreams, your young men shall see visions.

I claimed this scripture so that she would be born again and baptized in the Holy Spirit. One day, when she was four years old, Sarah said, "Mother, after you put me to bed tonight, I will wake up, and God is going to baptize me with the Holy Spirit, and I am going to pray in tongues." I thought, "Well, she's heard this in Sunday School, and she's saying it because she knows that it will please me." But I didn't say that to her; instead I said, "Sarah, that will be wonderful!"

When I put her to bed, Sarah fell asleep immediately. Later when I looked in on her, she was sitting up in her bed smiling, praying in tongues! I had marked her to receive what God had destined for her—the gift of the Holy Spirit.

MARK YOUR CHILDREN FOR GOD

Marking our children for God is nothing new. Hannah marked her child for God even before she became pregnant (1 Samuel 1:11; Also, see 1 Samuel 1:2–2:21):

And she vowed a vow, and said, O LORD of hosts, if thou wilt . . . give unto thine handmaiden a man child, then I will give him unto the LORD all the days of his life . . .

I really admire Hannah's faith. She could easily have become discouraged and depressed being married to Elkanah; he had another wife, Peninnah, who had children. But Hannah had been unable to conceive, and she bore the shame of her barrenness with a heavy heart. Hannah prayed and wept bitterly before the Lord.

Perhaps you, or someone you know, desires to conceive a child, but the doctors have said it is impossible. I want to encourage you because when Wally and I got married, we wanted to have children, but we were told that we couldn't have a baby. Every doctor I visited told me I had inherited sterility problems; and therefore, it was impossible for me to have a baby.

I have to admit, my faith wavered, but not Wally's. One day I asked him, "How does your faith remain so firm?" He answered, "Because I have the faith of Jesus, Marilyn." Thirteen years after we were married, I gave birth to a lovely, baby girl.

Sarah certainly was our miracle baby, and we marked her life according to God's goals for His children. She has grown into a lovely, young woman—born again, and Spirit-filled. Sarah graduated from Oral Roberts University and used to teach at our Christian school. One summer she went to China and taught Chinese students to speak German. (If I sound like a proud momma, it's because I am.)

Hannah also had gone to the Lord and said, "Lord, if You will give me a son, I will give him back to You, and he will serve You all the days of his life." God remembered Hannah. She and her husband had a son and named him *Samuel* which means "heard of God." Samuel's mother really had marked his life with a godly goal, to be a servant unto the Lord.

Did you know that when we dedicate our children to God, we actually are marking them for God's service? And, by faith, we also can mark our children before they are conceived. We can pray, "Father, I thank You for the children that I will bring into this world. I am asking You to bless them, and I am claiming them for Your kingdom. They are not going to waiver to the right nor to the left, but they will serve You forever."

What are we doing? We are saying, "God, I set myself in agreement with the eternal goals that You have set for my children's lives. I am going to pray, witness, and instruct them according to Your Word and trust You for the rest" (see Proverbs 22:6).

That's what Hannah did—she raised Samuel according to the Word of God. And at the appointed time, Hannah took Samuel to study under the high priest Eli. It couldn't have been easy for Samuel living with Eli, because Eli definitely was not a very godly man. He certainly hadn't marked his children because they were the absolute pits! Nevertheless, it was necessary for Samuel to live in that atmosphere.

Doesn't this bring to mind the terrible temptations that our children are faced with today at the school they attend, on the television programs they want to watch, and in the music they prefer? That's why we Christian parents must begin to Satan-proof our children by marking them for God at an early age. I believe that part of the reason why Samuel did not backslide—despite all the sin around him—was because his mother had marked him for God. Hannah literally Satan-proofed Samuel, and today we can do the same for our children.

MARK YOUR CHILDREN WITH PRAYER

One summer a friend wrote and shared that she had lost her husband to a woman who was involved in witchcraft. The husband also had moved their sons in with this woman for four months. Satan really wanted to get a big victory out of the husband's sin, but:

"God protected them [her sons] through my prayers and through the prayers of many other people. And praise God they are now back with me and have accepted Jesus into their hearts. They are doing beautifully now."

This mother marked her children; she refused to allow the devil to steal her children! How? With fervent prayer:

. . . *The effectual fervent prayer of a righteous man availeth much* (James 5:16).

The word *fervent* can mean "heated to the welding point"—that's white hot! With her white-hot prayers, this tenacious woman had welded her will to what God had destined for her sons, and the devil had to take his hands off!

If I were to ask you who prayed for your salvation, many of you would answer, "My mother or grandmother." They marked you for what God had destined for you to receive—salvation and the baptism of the Holy Spirit.

I love what Kenneth Copeland shared when he was here at our church one time. He told us that, at one time, he had been uptight with God. He said, "God, You deal with me about every little thing I do. Other ministries get away with things, but You are always on my back." The Lord spoke back to him, "The reason I am always on your back is because your mother is on My back!" Kenneth Copeland's mother was praying white-hot prayers on his behalf, keeping him in the place where he could do what God had destined him to do.

Have you ever heard Kenneth Copeland's testimony? He was a young man who was as wild and rebellious as anyone I've ever heard of. He even rode a motorcycle down the halls of his high school because he saw his movie idol do it. Ken soon became involved in drugs, drinking, smoking, and the whole mess! But when he would come home at two or three o'clock in the morning, can you guess what his mother was doing? You guessed it, she was on her knees—marking her son for God's service. She said, "God, my son is marked. It doesn't matter what is going on around him. I have marked Ken for You, and he is not going to get away!"

Her white-hot prayers kept God's attention focused on her son. God turned Kenneth Copeland's life around, and he has become a powerful man of God.

Similarly, Hannah's white-hot prayers moved God to remember her, and she became pregnant with Samuel (1 Samuel 1:19–20). I believe Hannah continued to pray white-hot prayers for Samuel while he was with Eli. Undoubtedly Samuel knew he was marked and began to know the voice of God at a very young age:

. . . *the LORD called Samuel: and he answered, Here am I* (1 Samuel 3:4).

Therefore, just as marking Samuel worked for Hannah, marking Kenneth Copeland worked for his mother, marking our children worked for Wally and me, so will marking your children work for you!

The prophet Jeremiah also had been marked:

Before I formed thee in the belly I knew thee; and before thou camest forth out of the womb I sanctified thee, and I ordained thee a prophet unto the nations (Jeremiah 1:5).

The word *sanctify* means "to set apart." Doesn't that sound familiar? Remember *destine* also means "to set apart." God had destined Jeremiah to serve Him in the office of a prophet.

You know, I get so angry when I think about abortion. This truly is the most heinous crime ever committed against children. My heart weeps for the millions of babies killed and for their mothers, who (afterwards) suffer terrible emotional trauma!

The Bible clearly shows that God has destined us before the foundation of the world to be made into His image, yet misguided people are deceiving themselves into believing that abortion is an acceptable form of birth control. I firmly believe this horrendous practice has brought a curse upon our country.

Certainly, God loves women; and, of course, we have rights! But God also loves babies. We absolutely have no right to determine which babies should live or die, because all people are marked by God to receive eternal life (through repentance and the new birth) and to receive the baptism of the Holy Spirit.

Folks, there is absolutely no question; abortion is murder, and we Christians need to begin protecting our own sons and daughters against the possibility of being tricked by this devious lie of the devil. We need to begin Satan-proofing our children, grandchildren, and great-grandchildren until Jesus comes. We need to mark them for God and pray white-hot prayers on their behalf!

What if Jeremiah's mother had aborted him? We would have missed one of the greatest prophets of all time. And look at the apostle Paul:

But when it pleased God, who separated me from my mother's womb, and called me by his grace, To reveal his Son in me, that I might preach him among the heathen . . . (Galatians 1:15–16).

When had Paul been marked? While he was still in his mother's womb—just like Jeremiah had been centuries before. Now I want to show you that even though we sometimes stray away from what God has destined for us, God will continue to deal with us until we come in line with His will for our lives.

Paul started out, not as an immoral person who was involved in what we would call overt sin, but someone who had a horrible attitude that was totally unlike God. Paul was a legalist, a Pharisee. Even though Paul had been marked to preach the gospel of Jesus Christ, Paul did everything he could to destroy Christians.

Paul was on his way to Damascus, to persecute more Christians, when he had a tremendous encounter with Christ Jesus. God knocked Paul to the ground and really got his attention. And God let Paul know that he had been marked, "Paul, you are My marked man. Now get up and go forward and serve Me." (see Acts 9:3–5,15).

Paul did just that, and, other than Christ Himself, Paul became the greatest apostle the world has ever known. Because of Paul's obedience to God, the door to salvation was opened to the Gentile world—that's you and me! And Paul wrote at least fourteen books in the New Testament. God had destined Paul to be in His service, and God certainly did not allow Paul to escape from his calling.

There is a beautiful woman on my staff who, at a very young age, got into a sinful lifestyle including drug abuse and immorality. Then her sister got saved and prayed for this woman. She eventually became born again and Spirit-filled. God delivered her from drugs and led her to Denver where she has continued to develop into a beautiful Christian wife and mother. She has worked very hard and has moved into an administrative position in my ministry. How did this happen? I believe this staff member's sister Satan-proofed and marked her; by praying white-hot prayers, she welded herself to God's will for her sister's life.

THE MARK OF FAITH

I want to tell you about a man who was born during a time when Egypt's Pharaoh had commanded that all male babies be thrown into the Nile River! Did you guess I was talking about Moses? But Moses' parents, Amram and Jochebed, refused to allow their precious son to be drowned or eaten by crocodiles:

By faith Moses, when he was born, was hid three months of his parents . . . they were not afraid of the king's commandment (Hebrews 11:23).

Rather they hid Moses for three months; then they put him in a basket and sent the basket floating down the river where Moses ended up in Pharaoh's daughter's bathtub! I love what Pharaoh's daughter said when she unwrapped Moses, "Oh, this is a Hebrew child" (see Exodus 2:6). How did she know that Moses was a Hebrew? His parents had marked Moses with circumcision which was God's mark for His covenant people.

I believe that when the devil looks at a Christian's child, he should say, "Oh no! This is a Christian's kid who has been marked for God's service. I am not going to waste my time here because I know this kid has been Satan-proofed by the white-hot prayers of his or her parents!"

When we study Hebrews 11, we see that it talks about Moses' faith. Why did Moses have so much faith? Because his parents had set the mark of faith upon him.

If you want to Satan-proof your children, then mark their lives with faith. Let them see you living by faith, reading God's Word, praying, and attending church. When you emphasize the importance of serving God, your children will think it's important too. They may not want to serve God right off the bat—but just hang in there, God will bring them through.

I want to encourage you to stop murmuring about your church in front of your children. Some of you go to church and on the way home you'll say, "Well, the greeters weren't too friendly," or "I really didn't like the message today," or "the pastor is too loud when he worships." Then you wonder why your children do not want to go to church. You've marked them with negative words. If you want to Satan-proof your children and mark them for God's service, then you'd better begin to speak well of your church so your children will esteem it too.

IT'S NEVER TOO LATE

I know that many of you are saying, "Well, Marilyn, I accepted Jesus as my Savior at a late age in life. My children have grown up. It's too late." Let me assure you, it's never too late. My mother became a Christian when I was 19, and that's when she began to mark my brother and me. The first thing she did was to put Bibles on all the end tables and coffee tables. Then she put up scriptures on the refrigerator door and around the sink—you should have seen our bathroom. All around the house we read scriptures like, *"Marvel not that I said unto thee, Ye must be born again"* (John 3:7). What was my mother doing? She was marking us for God.

It doesn't matter whether you are a 25-year-old parent or a 95-year-old parent—begin to Satan-proof your children by marking them with God's Word (and don't forget those white-hot prayers). Your children may think you are a little crazy, but that's all right; mark them anyway!

Psalm 127:3–5 says:

Lo, children are an heritage of the LORD: and the fruit of the womb is his reward. As arrows are in the hand of a mighty man; so are children of the youth. Happy is the man that hath his quiver full of them: they shall not be ashamed, but they shall speak with the enemies in the gate.

Your children are your arrows, and they will go in the direction that you point them. That is why the book of Proverbs instructs Christian parents to train our children in the way they should go. When our children grow up, they won't depart from that training. Oh, they may stray for a while, but eventually they will return to godly ways.

When you train your children according to God's Word, you are marking their direction. You're making them into straight arrows who will *"speak with the enemies in the gate."* What does that mean? It means when we mark our children, we actually are training them to stand against the devil. If Jesus tarries, most of us will die, and our children are going to have to be able to deal with Satan. Ask yourself, "Am I preparing my children to stand against the fiery darts of the enemy?"

Do you remember what God said about Abraham before Isaac was born?

For I know him, that he will command his children and his household after him, and they shall keep the way of the LORD, to do justice and judgment; that the LORD may bring upon Abraham that which he has spoken of him (Genesis 18:19).

Abraham knew how important it was to teach his children about God. He knew that they needed to be marked, and his son Isaac certainly knew and served God. It's so important that you teach your children to serve God. I want to show you four ways that you can mark your children: through discipline, through instruction, by not provoking them to wrath, and by treating them like your heavenly Father treats you.

When we think about disciplining our children, we Christians have to throw out what we have heard from secular psychologists who said, "Don't discipline the little darlings. Let them be free to express themselves in whatever way they desire." That kind of counsel produced kids who swung from the chandeliers, broke windows, pulled down draperies, and everything else. In contrast, Christians must obey God's Word:

The rod and reproof give wisdom: but a child left to himself bringeth his mother to shame (Proverbs 29:15).

Now don't say, "Marilyn Hickey said I should beat my kids." I am not saying that, but certainly godly discipline will sometimes require parents to spank their children. Another way to mark your children is by teaching them. You say, "I bring them to Sunday School and to the midweek youth service." But really, is 2½ hours a week enough instruction to prepare a child to stand against the wiles of the devil? I don't believe so. Our children must be taught the Word of God on a daily basis, and they also need to be prayed with regularly.

There is something else about marking our children. Paul wrote in Ephesians 6:4:

And, ye fathers, provoke not your children to wrath: but bring them up in the nurture and admonition of the Lord.

Of course, we are to discipline our children; but while we are correcting and shaping their wills, we must be careful not to break their spirits. The most important thing you can give your children is a good self-image. When your children need reproving, do it; but say, "I know you have misbehaved, and I am going to correct you by punishing you. But I love you, and I have confidence that you will not do this again." Always build them up.

A soft answer turneth away wrath: but grievous words stir up anger. . . . A wholesome tongue is a tree of life: but perverseness therein is a breach of the spirit (Proverbs 15:1–4).

You can keep Satan from taking over your child's emotions

during times of correction by speaking wholesome words. Criticism should always be constructive; and remember, the ratio of encouragement to constructive criticism should be 90 percent encouragement to 10 percent criticism.

Another thing I want to share about marking your children is that we really need to treat them like God treats us. You say, "Marilyn, I don't know if I can handle that." I know you can't in the natural; however, you have a new nature—you are being conformed to the image of Christ—so that makes you supernatural.

Let's see how God treats people: He is quick to forgive us; He loves us unconditionally; He never forsakes us; He is merciful and compassionate toward us; and He instructs us. In Christ you can treat your children with the same love and concern that God has for you.

The last thing I want to say about marking your household has to do with believers living with unsaved mates. Some of you get so out of it when it comes to your unsaved husband or wife. It's almost as if you suspect that your mate may be the devil himself! But did you know that God calls your unsaved husband or wife "the elect?"

Therefore I endure all things for the elect's sakes, that they may also obtain the salvation which is in Christ Jesus with eternal glory (2 Timothy 2:10).

Paul was saying that he would endure all things for the sake of people who had not yet received salvation. And all men are destined to come to repentance and be born again—that includes your unsaved loved one.

The Bible also says that one believing mate sanctifies—sets

apart, marks, or calls God's attention to the entire household. So don't get so excited because your spouse is unsaved. Just keep on Satan-proofing your loved ones and marking your household for God. Keep praying in the Holy Spirit—sending God those white-hot prayers. Keep allowing the love of Jesus to be shed abroad in your home. Keep speaking God's promises on your spouse's behalf; and above all, stay in faith that God will move on His promises and do His perfect work in your loved one's life.

CHAPTER SIX

SOWING AND REAPING MIRACLES

What is a miracle? The dictionary defines *a miracle* as "an effect or extraordinary event in the physical world that surpasses all known human or natural powers and is ascribed to a supernatural cause." Miracles usually cause quite a stir in the lives of unbelievers—they have such a difficult time accepting that there is an almighty God, Who sometimes upsets the natural order of things and performs miracles.

But we, in the Body of Christ, know that when our heavenly Father performs a miracle—something beyond human or natural powers—He simply is making His presence known in the world. Therefore, believers should accept miracles as a normal part of our existence. In this chapter, I'm going to show you how you can experience God's miracle-working power when you begin to sow miracles into the lives of others.

Sometimes I wonder why so few Christians experience the marvelous, miracle-working power of God in their lives.

Walking in the miraculous should be a normal everyday activity for Christians. Contrary to what many of you may think, miracles are not limited to the lives of people you believe to be "super Christians." Miracles occur in the lives of ordinary believers, like you and me, who have been empowered by an extraordinary God to accomplish supernatural things.

When you received Christ as your Savior, you literally became a miracle. By the power of God, you entered a new realm—a supernatural realm where the impossible becomes possible because of faith. What faith? Your faith in Jesus Christ that allows you to stand on and to live according to every Word that comes forth from the mouth of God:

But ye shall receive power, after that the Holy Ghost is come upon you . . . (Acts 1:8).

God's Word says believers will receive power. The Greek word here for *power* is *dunamis* which means "miraculous power, ability, strength, violence, and abundance." We get our word "dynamite" from the word *dunamis.* God's *dunamis*—miracle-working power—operating in your life will give you the ability to rise up strong in the Holy Spirit. You will become an explosive force in the spiritual realm.

If you are a Spirit-filled believer, then God's miracle-working power is within you. As a Satan-proofer you are the recipient of an "extraordinary-ness" that surpasses all known human or natural powers—the Holy Spirit. There is another word for *power* that I want to look at:

Behold, I give unto you power to tread on serpents and scorpions, and over all the power of the enemy: and nothing shall by any means hurt you (Luke 10:19).

In this scripture, the power of the enemy is miracle-working power. The Bible gives many examples of demonic miracles being performed, beginning when the serpent spoke with Eve:

... *And he* [the serpent] *said unto the woman, Yea, hath God said, Ye shall not eat of every tree of the garden?* (Genesis 3:1).

Can you imagine yourself having a conversation with a snake? That certainly would qualify as an extraordinary event that surpassed all known human powers—a miracle. What about when Moses went before Pharaoh? The Egyptian sorcerers performed almost exactly the same miracles as did Moses—their rods became serpents; they caused the waters in the Nile River to turn to blood; and they caused frogs to come forth in a plague (Exodus 7:12,22; 8:7). These events, although extraordinary happenings, definitely were not caused by God.

Now look back at Luke 10:19 where it says power to tread on serpents and scorpions. Here the Greek word used for *power* is *exousia* which means "authority."

Satan's miracle-working power absolutely pales when compared to the authority of God. God has given authority and miracle-working power to believers—to step all over the devil! And there is no question that when you begin to sow miracles into the lives of others, you are going to have to step on the devil's toes.

You received God's authority the moment you were born again; and if you have been baptized in the Holy Spirit, you have been given God's miracle-working power. So, when you think about Satan-proofing your household by sowing miracles, I want you to know that God absolutely has equipped you to handle this challenge; through Christ Jesus, you can do it!

OFF WITH THE OLD . . . ON WITH THE NEW

As I said earlier, Christians should be involved in the miraculous as a normal occurrence. What stops us? I believe God's power operating in our lives is hindered when we become tangled up in our old nature. For various reasons, we sometimes harbor negative thoughts, attitudes, or emotions like unforgiveness, bitterness, anger, or resentment. These things are products of our old nature, and believe me, they will stop God's miracle-working power from flowing freely in our lives.

I want to talk to you about your emotions. Sometimes it is so easy to become negative. My heart almost breaks when I hear about the terrible suffering that some of you have experienced at the hands of others. You have reason to be angry and hurt—these are normal emotional responses.

But did you know that your emotions provide one of Satan's favorite playgrounds? An emotional response to a situation may be normal, but Satan can invade your emotions. Before you know it, that normal response may turn into a sinful condition: *Be angry, and sin not . . . Neither give place to the devil* (Ephesians 4:26–27).

If you want to sow miracles into the lives of others, then you will need to Satan-proof your emotions. God knows that sometimes you may become angry; but if you allow Satan to inflate your emotions, your anger may turn into hate. There are times when you may experience disappointment. If you aren't careful, Satan can intensify your feelings and you may become severely depressed and discouraged.

But remember all these negative things are part of our old

nature, and we cannot experience God's miracle-working power in that condition. God wants us all to be Satan-proofers and to overcome our old nature so we can operate in our new nature on a consistent basis. That's when believers really begin to walk in the miraculous. I want to tell you about a bona fide Satan-proofer who literally sowed miracles into her enemy's life.

Years ago, a woman in our city came to me and shared how her daughter—a Bible-school student in her thirties—had been stabbed to death! What a horrible tragedy! The mother told me how she had gone into a deep depression because of her over-whelming grief. She soon became bitter toward God and built up a tremendous hatred for the murderer, who, after taking the lives of many more women, had finally been apprehended.

One Saturday night God spoke to my friend and said, "If you don't forgive that murderer, I cannot forgive you because if you don't forgive the trespasses of others, I can't forgive you of yours." Maybe she felt she had a right to be angry and hurt, but God insisted that she forgive the man.

So, this dear lady reached out to God; and by faith, she for-gave her daughter's murderer. The next day God gave her an opportunity to act out her faith; and in doing so, she sowed a miracle into the man's life. The Gideons came to her church, and she made a contribution for Bibles. Then she asked one of the Gideons to go and present a Bible personally to her daughter's murderer, who was in prison.

YES, you know what happened. God performed a miracle in that vicious killer's heart, and he became a victorious Christian. He literally became a missionary in that prison!

The woman sowed another miracle into this man's life and paid for his correspondence Bible school material. One day she said to me, "Marilyn, the devil murdered my daughter, who was going to be a missionary; but God, in His great mercy, took my daughter's murderer and made him a missionary in a place where my daughter could never go!" Folks, THIS IS A MIRACLE!

How did it happen? This woman certainly had the right to be angry and hurt. This man had brutally murdered her daughter! Whether knowingly or unknowingly, he had allowed himself to be used by the devil and had harmed many people. But did my friend allow Satan to turn her anger into hate? NO! She sowed a miracle into this man's life and reaped a tremendous miracle in her own—the peace that passes all understanding over her daughter's death. That was extraordinary and certainly surpassed all human powers!

My friend took authority over any evil effort that the devil wanted to exert in her emotions. By faith she stepped out of the realm of her emotions and into the realm of the supernatural—the miraculous! By doing so, she became a conduit for God's authority and miracle-working power to flow into the murderer's life. These miracles probably wouldn't have occurred if the woman had been operating according to her emotions. She sowed a miracle, and miracles continue to multiply each time another prisoner gets saved.

We all need to Satan-proof our emotions. Friends, let me say that one of the many roadblocks the devil will use to hinder you from receiving God's miracles is to keep you operating in your emotions—your old nature. However, through Christ Jesus, you have been given God's authority to step out of the realm of your emotions into the realm of the supernatural—your new nature.

In your new nature you will sow blessings and miracles even into the lives of your enemies. After all, in terms of people, your enemies are just victims, who, either knowingly or unknowingly, have allowed the devil to manipulate them into hurting you. When you begin to bless and sow miracles in the lives of these people, then you will begin to walk in the miraculous on a more consistent basis in your own life.

You say, "Scripture says I have authority to tread on serpents and scorpions. I thought that meant the devil, not my emotions." You're right! But the devil can magnify your emotions to a very negative level; and if you aren't careful, your emotions can easily get out of control and you'll end up in a sinful condition.

My friend could have allowed the devil to invade her emotions and turn the normal grieving process into bitterness. There isn't a deadlier sting than the results of a life lived in anger. And just as the poison from a snake (serpent) can destroy you, so can bitterness and anger destroy your relationships, hopes, and dreams.

Let me encourage you who have had painful experiences with another person: you must begin to Satan-proof your emotions, keeping in mind that your heavenly Father is *El Shaddai*, "the Lord Who is more than enough." His Holy Spirit in you makes you more than enough to overcome any negative feelings or thoughts that you may be harboring against someone. You will no longer focus on the terrible thing that may have been done to you. Instead, you'll focus on Jesus Christ and begin to operate in your new nature. Christ in you will take you out of the ordinary into the extraordinary, and you'll respond to your adversaries with love. It's your attitude toward people that determines your altitude in the miracle-working power of God.

I believe we have probably all had occasions where a person has verbally, emotionally, or physically abused us. And if something bad happens to the person, we may think, "Goody, goody! That's what they deserve." I know some of you have felt that way at one time or another, and sometimes I have too. But that's really an ugly attitude, straight out of our old nature:

Rejoice not when thine enemy falleth, and let not thine heart be glad when he stumbleth: Lest the LORD see it, and it displease him . . ." (Proverbs 24:17–18).

This verse does not refer to our real enemy the devil, but to people who harm us. Regardless what the circumstances may be, God says, "I know how you feel; but don't rejoice in another's catastrophes, it will displease Me."

The Bible is quite clear when it talks about how we are to treat our enemies. Jesus said:

But I say unto you, Love your enemies, bless them that curse you, do good to them that hate you, and pray for them which despitefully use you, and persecute you (Matthew 5:44).

We are to love, bless, pray, and do good for them—we are to sow miracles into the lives of our enemies. Now, your old nature doesn't want to do these things; but your new nature, the one you received when you were born again, wants to do good for all people.

God wants to set you free from wrong thinking and wrong attitudes that come out of your old nature. God wants you to become a Satan-proofer and get out of the realm of your emotions so you can reach into the supernatural and pull down miracles for your life and for others as well.

MIRACLES IN YOUR EMOTIONS

Many of you are thinking right now, "I just can't control my emotions." But that simply is not true, because in Christ you can do all things (see Philippians 4:13). The Bible contains many examples of believers who chose to serve God rather than their emotions—they are not all big names like Jesus, Elijah, Moses, or Paul either. Some of their names are not even mentioned. For instance, Naaman's wife's handmaiden.

At one time in Israel's history, Syria had repeatedly come down and attacked God's people. One of the major leaders in the Syrian army was a man named Naaman (see 2 Kings 5:1). On one of his campaigns against Israel, the Syrians had taken captive a little Jewish girl who had become a servant to his wife.

Imagine the emotional tearing this young girl must have experienced being kidnapped from her home and forced into slavery by the Syrians. Then one day she learned that her mistress' husband had the dreaded disease leprosy. It must have been difficult for her to resist the urge to rejoice at Naaman's calamity and say, "He stole me from my parents, church, and life. He deserves to have leprosy because he killed a lot of my relatives!" But she didn't rejoice; instead, she said to her mistress:

. . . Would God my lord were with the prophet that is in Samaria! for he would recover him of his leprosy (2 Kings 5:3).

I want to compare Naaman's servant's response with the

response of a woman who was forced to endure a different kind of slavery. One of my Bible school students shared that from the age of seven to the age of sixteen, she had been sexually abused by her step-mother's brother. Many times, she went to her parents and told them how she had been enslaved to this man's sickening behavior, but they didn't believe her. Inevitably, she became pregnant; and, through some very painful circumstances, she miscarried her child.

I praise God that this young woman eventually got out of that abusive environment, and now she is born again and Spirit-filled. She has done missionary work in Africa, Japan, Korea, and the Virgin Islands; and she has a tremendous desire to become involved in a prayer ministry. It took time, but God has healed her emotionally and physically from the damage inflicted upon her while she was growing up.

However, one day her step-uncle injured himself when he fell from a ladder. The doctors said he would never walk again. Now watch how God performed a miracle in this situation. If the young woman had allowed herself to operate from her old nature, she could have really rejoiced at the calamity of the man who had destroyed her precious childhood. Instead she sowed a miracle into his life, and she forgave her abuser! Then she led him to the Lord! Now he, his wife, and most of their children are saved and serving God!

Quite honestly, most of us want to see God's miracles occurring in our own lives, but we rarely want to sow miracles into the lives of other people—especially the lives of our enemies. But let me tell you, sowing and reaping and asking for miracles go together like Siamese twins. Look at what happened when Naaman's little Jewish servant resisted the urge to snicker and gloat over Naaman's mishap. She sowed a miracle into Naaman's life by suggesting that he go and see the prophet Elisha. Naaman visited Elisha and was miraculously healed of leprosy. But he wasn't just healed of the disease, the greater miracle occurred in Naaman's heart:

And he returned to the man of God, he and all his company, and came, and stood before him: and he said, Behold, now I know that there is no God in all the earth, but in Israel . . . (2 Kings 5:15).

Naaman is never mentioned again as one who led an attack against Israel. Why? Because his life was changed, and he no longer was Israel's enemy:

When a man's ways please the LORD, he maketh even his enemies to be at peace with him (Proverbs 16:7).

Naaman probably went back to Syria and presented himself before his king and gave a tremendous testimony! But the Syrian king didn't seem to be impressed by the miracle-working power of the God of Israel.

You know, sometimes we believers get into a similar mindset. We can see God's wonderful miracle-working power in action in someone else's life but refuse to accept miracles in our own lives. One man in our church found it difficult to believe that divine healing flowed so easily through our congregation. He didn't believe that people could be in severe pain one moment and be completely pain free the next.

Then he injured his leg. When he came to church, his leg was swollen, blue, and throbbing with pain. The Holy Spirit led us into a healing service, and you guessed it—our friend who was in severe pain one moment was completely pain free the next.

Nevertheless, God's miracle-working power didn't affect the Syrian king. He continued to attack Israel again and again. However, his armies never succeeded in surprising the Israelites—they always seemed to know when and where their enemy was going to attack. It would have been natural for the Syrian king to assume there was a traitor in his camp. He demanded to know, "Who is the dirty traitor?"

And one of his servants said, None, my lord, O king: but Elisha, the prophet that is in Israel, telleth the king of Israel the words that thou speakest in thy bedchamber (2 Kings 6:12).

Elisha certainly was a tremendous man of faith. By faith Elisha heard the king making secret plans to attack Israel—in the privacy of the royal bedroom! The Bible says:

The secret things belong unto the LORD our God: but those things which are revealed belong unto us . . . (Deuteronomy 29:29).

Because God knows the secret plots of men, He can lead us by His Spirit so we won't fall into the enemy's snares. I think sometimes we Christians believe if we don't bang our enemies around, our enemies will bang us around. But I am going to tell you that if you stay true to God, He will show you the secrets of your enemies and protect you from them. And what does God want you to do with what He reveals to you about your enemies? He wants you to bless them, pray for them, and sow miracles into their lives. All of this comes out of our new nature—our faith nature.

I received a letter from a woman in Dallas who wrote about how God dealt with her about being involved in an adult bookstore business. She terminated her involvement and then challenged her husband to do the same. He refused and chose to stay involved in pornography rather than to continue with his marriage to this courageous Christian lady. She said in her letter:

"While my husband and I were separated, he became acquainted with a girl who was a hooker and a cocaine addict. At first, I was angry, bitter, and really hurt. My prayers seemed to go unanswered."

Then one day:

"A voice spoke to me saying, 'Read about forgiveness.' . . . I prayed a prayer and spoke my husband's name first and then the girl's name, forgiving them both. The peace and love and joy I found and felt at that moment couldn't be described. It was truly the peace that passes all understanding. After that prayer, God began to open my eyes and heart for this girl. For 13 months I prayed for her; eating, sleeping, and breathing for her salvation."

Eventually the woman's marriage was restored, and the other woman ended up in prison. While she was imprisoned, this woman received Christ as her Savior and began witnessing to the guards and inmates!

Do you see what happened here? She was betrayed by her husband and injured by this other woman. She allowed the devil to invade the normal emotional reaction and escalate it into bitterness and resentment which was in her old nature. The minute that she got into her old nature, her prayers went unanswered.

Folks, as long as you are in your old nature, you will not experience God's miracle-working power in your life.

When this lady stepped out of the realm of her emotions and into the realm of the supernatural, God intervened in her situation and brought about a change. Was it an easy thing for her to accomplish? No, but in her new nature—the Christ-like nature—loving her enemy became possible.

DIVINE PROTECTION

When you begin to sow miracles into the lives of your enemies, don't be surprised when the devil really zeroes in on you. That Syrian king told his servants to find Elisha:

. . . Go and spy where he is, that I may send and fetch him. And it was told him saying, Behold, he is in Dothan (2 Kings 6:13).

Elisha was in the city of *Dothan*, which means "a double decree." When you sow miracles into the lives of other people, you'll get a double miracle—one in their lives and one in your life too.

I am always amazed that the Syrian king felt it necessary to send so many soldiers to capture Elisha:

Therefore sent he thither horses, and chariots, and a great host: and they came by night, and compassed the city about (2 Kings 6:14).

All these soldiers were trying to sneak up on Elisha in the middle of the night, but remember that God was revealing their plans to Elisha. Although he knew they were coming, do you think Elisha was nervous? No way! Elisha was operating in the supernatural realm—the faith realm. Now his servant was the one who had the problem. He was absolutely terrified.

Look at how lovingly Elisha dealt with his servant. Elisha didn't jump down his throat saying, "You're not supposed to be afraid. Haven't you been listening to what I have been teaching you?" Rather, Elisha sowed a miracle into his servant's life:

And Elisha prayed, and said, LORD, I pray thee, open his eyes, that he may see. And the LORD opened the eyes of the young man; and he saw: and, behold, the mountain was full of horses and chariots of fire round about Elisha (2 Kings 6:17).

Elisha prayed for a miracle, and prayer is the major means by which you are going to see God's miracle-working power flow into your life too. Elijah sowed a miracle through prayer, and this young servant saw the divine protection that God has for His people.

When the servant looked up, he saw that the mountain was full of horses and chariots of fire! Certainly, he recalled Elisha's testimony about how Elijah had been taken up in a chariot of fire. Now he was seeing firsthand that God's chariots of fire were there for Elisha too. Did you notice that Elisha didn't pray for himself to see God's divine protection? Elisha operated in a supernatural realm, and by faith he knew God's miracle-working power would work in his circumstances just as it had worked in Elijah's.

So many times when we are faced with new challenges, we need to keep in mind that the same God Who delivered us in the past certainly is able to deliver us in the present. Even though we may not always be able to see the end result, we can be certain that God's protection is around His people. The Bible asks a very profound question:

. . . *If God be for us, who can be against us?* (Romans 8:31).

The answer, of course, is NO ONE! There will always be more standing for God's people than against them. Look at Elisha; the Syrians had surrounded his house. Can you imagine a whole army coming to get one little man? I think that is almost funny. The king of Syria obviously was afraid of Elisha.

Did you know that the devil is afraid of you? One little Christian frightens Satan silly. He knows that when you begin to operate in your new nature—your faith nature—and begin to walk by the authority and the miracle-working power of God— then he has had it!

Elisha prayed for another miracle:

. . . *Smite this people, I pray thee, with blindness. And he smote them with blindness according to the word of Elisha* (2 Kings 6:18).

Isn't it interesting that God opened the eyes of Elisha's servant, and then closed the eyes of Elisha's enemies? I think there have been times when God has closed the eyes of officials when my ministry team has taken the Word of God into communist countries.

One time we were taking Bibles into Poland. We also wanted to make a video, so we had 13 pieces of video equipment with us. We had been warned that the customs officers might confiscate our equipment when we got to Warsaw because the government didn't like the idea of Christians corning into their country making videos. However, we believed God was leading us; so, we prayed before we got off the plane, "Lord, help us to come through and get all our videos in and out quickly and safely—

even if you have to blind the eyes of the customs people."

The customs officer was a woman. She had an ugly attitude and really gave me a hard time. But when she saw my associate who had the 13 pieces of video equipment, she smiled so sweetly at him and told him to go through.

I don't believe she even saw the equipment. I believe God closed her eyes to the equipment that we needed to perform what He had called us to do in Poland.

Similarly, God had blinded the Syrian soldiers; then Elisha tricked them into going to Samaria the capital of Israel. When they arrived, Israel's king, Jehoram, said to Elisha:

. . . My father, shall I smite them? shall I smite them? (2 Kings 6:21).

Jehoram thought, "What an opportunity to kill all these Syrians. They are just like sitting ducks!" That was a natural response, but God's Word tells us to love our enemies. We are to pray for them, bless them, and do good to them. And don't forget; it was God's miracle-working power that had brought the enemy to the king's front door in the first place. Why did God do it? To show His marvelous mercy. You see the Lord is not only a friend to believers, He is also a friend to sinners. God has destined that all people would come to repentance so we all can be born again and Spirit-filled.

When Jehoram exposed his desire to kill the Syrians, Elisha answered:

…Thou shalt not smite them: wouldest thou smite those whom thou hast taken captive with thy sword and with thy bow? set bread and water before them, that they may eat and drink, and

go to their master (2 Kings 6:22).

Doesn't God's Word tell us that if our enemy is hungry, we are to feed him? To give him water if he is thirsty? If you can pray for your enemies and sow miracles into their lives, that in itself is a miracle. It means that you are a Satan-proofer doing extraordinary things that surpass human power. You'll be operating out of your new nature; and through Jesus Christ, you will accomplish the miraculous.

You know, if you are looking for a double feast of God's miracle-working power in your life, you must come out of your old nature. Elisha could have led those blind men right over the edge of a cliff; or he could have said to Jehoram, "Yes! Go ahead and kill them." That certainly would have been the natural thing to do.

However, Elisha was not operating in the natural; he was operating in the supernatural; and he showed forth God's marvelous mercies to Israel's enemies. They fed the Syrian army and sent them home.

That certainly must have been a huge grocery bill. But it always costs you something when you choose to walk in the miraculous and sow love, peace, joy, and righteousness into the lives of others. Salvation is free, but serving the Lord will cost you something. Do you know what it costs? It costs you your old nature, which really isn't a terribly big price to pay in order to see God's wonderful miracles occurring in your life on a more consistent basis.

CHAPTER SEVEN

WISDOM FOR YOUR FUTURE

I really get inspired when I read the book of Hebrews. Chapter 11 is sometimes referred to as the "Hall of Fame" for our biblical faith heroes. It absolutely overflows with examples of ordinary people who walked in godly wisdom. They put their faith in an extraordinary God and supernaturally Satan-proofed their future.

Through the lives of Abraham, Isaac, Jacob, and Joseph, we are going to see how we can walk in godly wisdom and, by faith, secure our future. You may say, "Marilyn, I want to secure my family's future, but I don't know how to get godly wisdom."

If any of you lack wisdom, let him ask of God, that giveth to all men liberally, and upbraideth not; and it shall be given to him (James 1:5).

The Greek word used here for *wisdom* means "a clarity in spiritual things." In order to secure your future, you need to get a better understanding of the things of God. You need to know how to secure your future according to God's plan for your life; that means you'll have to seek what God has planned for you and your loved ones.

We live in a time of uncertainty—in our personal lives as

well as in the world. Some people live in a constant state of fear because they focus on the statistics on crime, abortion, and substance abuse, which continue to increase at an alarming rate. Many times, they have experienced firsthand the heartbreaking results of the demise of God's first established institution—marriage. People look at all the unrest in the world, and they desperately wonder, "Oh dear, what's going on? Things are getting worse and worse. What will become of us?"

Praise God! Why? Because in the midst of all this chaos, you, the believer, don't have to worry! You are a covenant child of El Elyon, the Most High God. You can have the highest confidence because God has big plans for your future. However, you're going to have to begin walking in faith and in God's wisdom if you want to see His plans manifested in your future.

There are three blessings that we can look at when we talk about securing our future: material, inheritance, and victory. Despite the circumstances around you, God wants you to know that you, His child, have been blessed. When you live your life in an attitude of worship, you put yourself in a position to inherit everything that God has destined for you—eternal life, to be baptized into the Holy Spirit, and to be conformed into the wonderful image of Jesus Christ. In the image of Christ, you'll subdue the earth (your environment) and bear the fruit that accompanies victorious life (good health, financial security, and peace of mind).

Some of you may think, "Well, I'm born again. I love the Lord. But my health is bad, my finances are a mess, and my nerves are just about shot!" Do you wonder why you don't seem to be able to get it together and to walk in prosperity like other Christians? Be encouraged, because, although that may be where you are today, I believe when you begin to walk in faith and godly wisdom your life, health, and finances are going to do a complete turnaround. Your future will be secured according to God's desires for your life, and God plans for you to be victorious over your circumstances.

GOD'S WORD IS HIS WISDOM

As you begin to focus more intently on God's will for you and your loved ones and begin more seriously to seek God through prayer, Bible study, and the application of God's Word, then you'll start to become a Satan-proofer. And there absolutely is no question, your life will change and your future will be secured in God's Word.

Again, the key to a secured future is walking in godly wisdom. Let's get very practical. What do you do after you have prayed and asked God for wisdom? You spend a lot of time with God, and He will show you exactly how to apply the Scriptures to your circumstances. That's how you begin to secure your future by faith and godly wisdom.

By faith Isaac blessed Jacob and Esau . . . Jacob . . . blessed both the sons of Joseph . . . Joseph . . . made mention of the departing of the children of Israel; and gave commandment concerning his bones (Hebrews 11:20–22).

All these men secured their future by faith! Where did they put their faith? In God. And when they began to step out in His Word and His wisdom, they secured the future for themselves and for their loved ones.

I believe Abraham had a pretty clear understanding of spiritual things. When he walked in godly wisdom, Abraham secured the future for himself, his descendants, and the world. Abraham is sometimes called the "Father of Faith." There is no question that he was a man of supernatural faith. But even though he had faith, Abraham did not always walk in godly wisdom; and the results were disastrous.

Abraham acted in great faith when he first encountered God. And God instructed Abraham to leave his home in Haran and to travel to an unknown destination. Can you imagine the conversation that may have occurred between Abraham and Sarah that night?

"Sarah, God told me to leave Haran."

"'All right, Abraham, but where are we going?"

"Oh, I don't know. God didn't say. But He did say that in me would all the families of the earth be blessed" (see Genesis 12:1–3):

So Abram departed, as the LORD had spoken unto him . . . Abram was seventy and five years old when he departed out of Haran (Genesis 12:4).

When you think about this 75-year-old man and his household, you may be picturing some little band of nomads trudging off through the countryside. But, actually, Abraham had a huge household. He had many slaves, among them at least 318 trained soldiers and their wives and families (see Genesis 14:14). And this doesn't include Lot's household! So, when Abraham packed up his household and left Haran, he may have been leading a caravan of several thousand people.

At this point, I'm not sure how much godly wisdom Abraham walked in; but he certainly was wise enough to recognize and to obey God's instructions.

I love hearing testimonies from my former Bible school students and members of my staff. There are so many cases where God literally has called people to pack up and move to Denver. One of our pastors had called my husband and me to say he and his wife believed that God was calling them to Denver to become involved in our ministry. At that time there were no positions available, but they were convinced that Denver was in God's plan for their future.

So, we all prayed about it. Not long after that, an opening became available which was just tailor-made for their capabilities. They moved their family to Denver, and he now heads up our pastoral care ministry. This couple walked in God's wisdom for their future, and they have been such a tremendous blessing to us.

Now I want you to know that you will always have a choice as to whether you are going to walk wisely in spiritual things or not. This couple could have rationalized God's instructions to them about moving; after all, they pastored a thriving church in California. Similarly, Abraham could have said, "Oh, I'm just not sure; maybe that wasn't God's voice. I'd better stay here in Haran."

But Abraham didn't say that. He had tremendous faith in God, which really was supernatural because he had been an idolater. He didn't have a Bible, there were no church services—no evangelist came to Abraham's city to get him saved. No, it was God's spoken Word that convicted Abraham. Abraham stepped out on the Word and, by faith, secured the future not only for himself but also for all the people who depended upon him. Abraham served God, and he demanded that his entire household serve God along with him (see Genesis 18:19).

As I said earlier, Abraham was a man of great faith, but he didn't always walk in godly wisdom. There is a difference between walking in faith and walking in wisdom. One time after Abraham had been living in Canaan for about ten years, Sarah began to get nervous because she and Abraham hadn't conceived a child. She may have been thinking about God's promise that all the families on earth would be blessed through Abraham. How could that happen unless a child was born to Abraham? Then Sarah got an idea that she thought would speed up God's time-table. Evidently, the customs of the day allowed for an unusual way of conceiving an heir to whom one would leave their property. So, Sarah cooked up a scheme whereby Abraham would become sexually involved with Hagar, her Egyptian servant, and the child from that union would be Abraham's heir.

When Abraham heard the idea, he could have said, "No, Sarah. God didn't tell me to do things that way. We are going to trust God's Word to instruct us in our plans for the future." However, we know that Abraham went along with Sarah's kooky idea; and he and Hagar produced a son named Ishmael. I believe that Abraham and Sarah probably thought they had secured their future; but, actually, they were not operating in faith. They were operating in the flesh. Ishmael was not the promised seed; Isaac was.

Abraham did not walk in God's wisdom for that situation. He

may have had great faith to leave his homeland and to follow God into parts unknown, but faith without wisdom can cause big trouble for a believer.

The Bible indicates that about ten years passed before God communicated with Abraham again (see Genesis 17:1). This time God appeared to Abraham and told him to walk before Him and to be perfect. In other words, "Abraham, do things My way; and be sincere and upright in your walk."

It is imperative that we Christians do things God's way if we want to Satan-proof our lives and secure our future. As long as Abraham did things his way, disaster followed; but when he began to walk in faith and godly wisdom for his circumstances, blessings followed.

Abraham and Sarah finally got onto the right track. Together they had a son Isaac; however, the tension continued to grow between Sarah and Hagar until Abraham was forced to expel Hagar and his firstborn son, Ishmael, from his household. Sometimes I feel so sorry for Hagar and Ishmael. But then I know that God is so wonderful, and He loves all people. When Hagar and Ishmael began to cry out to God, He showed forth His marvelous mercies, and God secured their future with His provisions.

WISDOM FOR MATERIAL SECURITY

Abraham and Sarah raised Isaac according to God's Word. And, just before Abraham died, he blessed Isaac with his substance:

And Abraham gave all that he had unto Isaac (Genesis 25:5).

It's interesting that, despite having other sons by his concubine and by his second wife Keturah, Abraham gave all his wealth to Isaac. Abraham didn't ignore his other children—he gave them gifts, but he also sent them away from Isaac. Abraham's experience with Hagar and Ishmael probably taught him a lesson about strife—godly wisdom was employed to secure Isaac's future and to keep all his brothers from laying claim to Isaac's inheritance.

After Abraham died, God blessed Isaac and secured his future:

And it came to pass after the death of Abraham, that God blessed his son Isaac; and Isaac dwelt by the well Lahairoi (Genesis 25:11).

The Hebrew definition of *Lahairoi* means "a well of life." Isaac was really blessed, but who actually blessed his future? When Abraham was alive, he did all he could for his son, but it was God Who actually blessed Isaac's future. Abraham had sown the seeds—he prayed about Isaac and prepared his son to receive God's future plans. Although Abraham had claimed blessings for Isaac, it was God Who really gave life to Isaac's future.

One morning I was praying out on our back porch. I remember it was so pretty that summer, and it just seemed as if the Lord had opened up the heavens to me while I was praying. He asked me, "Did you know that when you pray, you are laying up treasures in heaven?" I thought, "Well, Father, I know we say that about our giving, but I didn't know about prayers." God went on to explain that when I prayed, it was as if I was depositing into a bank account. All the prayers I deposited would come down upon the people I had prayed for—blessings would come upon their lives as they drew out of my prayer account. I have seen some of the prayers come to pass; but, if Jesus tarries, some may not be manifested until after I die.

The prayers we pray in the present will bless people in the future. When believers are walking in godly wisdom, they have strong, consistent prayer lives. Prayer will bring you into a more intimate relationship with your heavenly Father, and God will share some wonderful revelations about how to apply His Word to your circumstances during those precious times of fellowship.

YOUR EXAMPLE CAN MAKE A DIFFERENCE

I want to look at Isaac's life to see if his future was secured by his father's blessings:

And Isaac was forty years old when he took Rebekah to wife . . . And Isaac intreated the LORD for his wife, because she was barren: and the LORD was intreated of him, and Rebekah his wife conceived (Genesis 25:20–21).

Doesn't this sound familiar? Isaac's mother had been barren, and now his wife Rebekah was barren. What did Isaac do? He interceded to God on Rebekah's behalf. No doubt Abraham and Sarah had shared their testimony again and again of how God had blessed them with their miracle baby, Isaac. They had secured Isaac's future by sharing their faith with him. When Isaac was confronted with a similar problem, he knew enough about spiritual things to pray and believe God for a child.

Allowing our children to see us walking diligently in faith and conducting our lives according to godly wisdom is the best example we can set because it sets the tone for their spiritual growth. You can see the principle of sowing and reaping in action here. If you sow spiritual things like faith and godly wisdom into your children's future, then they will reap a future rooted in faith and godly wisdom. However, when you sow worldly things like chance and luck, your children's future will be rooted in that same kind of instability.

We Christians must begin to Satan-proof our households and to prepare our children to live diligently in the wisdom of God. Yet we simply cannot pass along to our children what we do not have ourselves. So, if you need wisdom (and, quite frankly, we all do), ask God. Then begin to seek Him more through prayer and reading His Word. You will be pleasantly surprised at the difference godly wisdom makes in your life today—and in your future.

One of my favorite scriptures is:

But without faith it is impossible to please him: for he that cometh to God must believe that he is, and that he is a rewarder of them that diligently seek him (Hebrews 11:6).

I pray this scripture regularly during my prayer times. I have certain things that I am believing God for, but sometimes the answer (reward) seems to take forever. So, I continue to remind myself that God is a rewarder of them who diligently seek Him. When I set aside a daily time to spend with God, I know He is going to reward me for the time I spend with Him.

Maybe you need victory in your life, or perhaps your spouse or your children have some problem areas they need to overcome. Let me encourage you to be diligent in seeking God— that's wisdom! And when you continue to pray and trust God, He will reward you, and your family will be blessed to live victorious lives. Remember, diligence brings reward; lack of diligence brings nothing.

If you want to Satan-proof your loved ones, then you will

need to set aside a special time each day for prayer—genuine prayer that seeks God. Then not only will He reward you with His presence, but God also will bless you because you spent time seeking Him. Wow! That's a double-portion blessing! In addition, when you allow your children to see that spending time in God's presence is a primary part of your life, they too will begin to understand the importance of living in faith and walking in godly wisdom.

There is a woman I know who is such an inspiration because she has tremendous faith for the salvation of her loved ones. This woman is absolutely determined that her entire family is coming into the kingdom of God. She spends much time seeking God's wisdom, which she really needs because it takes godly wisdom to live with an unsaved mate.

This woman's bulldog faith secured her son's future when he was a senior in high school. All through his high school years, the young man had pretty much fooled around. Although he was very bright and was capable of getting good grades, he never quite hit the mark. Then in his last semester of school, the boy told his parents that he didn't really feel like going to school—he had given up hope of succeeding.

Despite his academic performance, my friend encouraged her son to stay in school—she was absolutely convinced of his ability to graduate with his class. She told him, "In Genesis, it says that all men are made in the image and likeness of God. Son, I don't care what anybody says about you. I choose right now to see the image of God in you. That's all I am going to look at."

This mother had faith in God for her son, and she walked in

godly wisdom and applied the Word to the situation. The young man decided to return to school, and God sent a Christian teacher to encourage him.

I believe this mother's supernatural faith secured her son's academic future because soon he began to have confidence in himself. He began to work diligently, carrying a full load plus one extra class; and he graduated from high school with his head held high.

The woman Satan-proofed her son by securing his future, and the results were victorious. In the future, if the boy should ever happen to become discouraged, I believe he will remember his mother's example; and God will bring him through difficult times again and again.

Let's look back at how Abraham's example of godly wisdom and faith took root in Isaac's life. When Isaac became old and was nearing death, he followed his father's example and blessed his children. I believe there is wisdom in blessing our children with our substance as well as with our mouths. So many parents have the attitude, "I never had it easy. I've always worked and earned my way. Let my children do the same."

I agree wholeheartedly that our children should be responsible for themselves, but I also know that we need to prepare our children to live independently. I believe it is very wise for parents to have insurance so their children will have the resources to pay for a college education in case the parents die. Educational security is an important part of securing the future for your children and your grandchildren.

Isaac saw the wisdom in his father's actions, and he wanted to do the same for his two sons Jacob and Esau. Isaac called Esau in and said, "Esau, go cook me some savory meat, because I want to bless you before I die" (see Genesis 27:4). Esau probably was very excited. He had already lost his birthright blessing through his own foolishness; and he had no intention of losing the firstborn blessing as well. So, he ran out to kill the meat he needed to make a stew for his aging father.

All this seems to be very much in order except for one thing. Isaac was not walking in godly wisdom. You only can operate in godly wisdom when you are living according to God's Word:

And the LORD said unto her, Two nations are in thy womb, and two manner of people shall be separated from thy bowels; and the one people shall be stronger than the other people; and the elder shall serve the younger (Genesis 25:23).

Blessing Esau was not what God had said to Rebekah. Rather, when these twin boys were still in her womb, God had said that the younger son would be blessed. The younger son was Jacob, not Esau; so, despite Isaac's seemingly good intentions, he simply was out of God's will. The firstborn blessing had to do with ruler-ship, prosperity, and priestly authority. Isaac was very unwise to try to secure the future of his household by choosing to give that blessing to Esau when God's choice was Jacob. Isaac's ungodly actions nearly resulted in his younger son's death, because Esau certainly wanted to kill Jacob.

Jacob had to flee for his life, and he went to live with his Uncle Laban. Poor Jacob had such a hard time. Laban changed Jacob's wages ten times and tricked him into marrying Leah when Jacob really loved Rachel. But one thing I noticed, Jacob always came out smelling like a rose!

Why? Because his father had secured his future by prophesying the blessings of God on Jacob's life. Folks, we can have faith for our children's future. When we, as parents, begin to walk in faith and to govern our actions by godly wisdom, then God's blessings will come upon our lives and our children's lives as well.

THE HARVEST

There is absolutely no question that you will reap what you sow. Maybe it will be a fast crop, and you'll reap it tomorrow or a month from now; or maybe your children will reap what you have sown long after your death. But you will always secure your future when you sow seeds of faith in God's Word. God's Word contains over 7,000 promises. And when God brings His Word to pass, there is always a harvest or manifestation of a promise.

One time a friend of ours was visiting from Pennsylvania. Sam is a pastor there, and he told me something so interesting. Sam comes from a Pennsylvania Dutch background. There were 12 children in his family. His parents were strict Mennonites.

Sam's mother was invited to a Pentecostal church and received the baptism of the Holy Spirit. She didn't quite know what to do because her husband was really involved with the Mennonite Church, and he would have been furious.

I love how godly wisdom leads us—this Spirit-filled mother began to pray secretly in tongues every day. She prayed for her family; then she invited them to attend the Pentecostal church. Six of her children were born again and Spirit-filled. Those six all graduated from Bible college and went into full-time ministry. How did this happen? Sam's mother walked in faith and godly wisdom, and the results were fantastic! She secured the future of her children and the future of thousands of people who will be touched by these full-time ministers.

Later Sam's father became ill with cancer. However, Sam's father had just gotten hold of the Word and he said, "I'm only 65. It's not time for me to die." God spoke to Sam's father and told him to prophesy and to bless all 12 of his children.

The doctors let him out of the hospital, and all of his children came to see him. They brought their wives and children, and it took 2½ hours for the man to prophesy what God had given him for each family member. Sam said, "Marilyn, our future is secure. We have been blessed by faith by our father."

Similarly, Jacob knew that his future was secure. Why? Because Isaac had blessed him. Despite the trickery involved, Jacob's future was secured when Isaac blessed him by faith. (Certainly, it was not by sight, because Isaac thought he was blessing Esau instead of Jacob.) This should give us all confidence to know that God will do all He possibly can to manifest His plans for our lives. Even if we don't have the perfect family, we can secure our future in God's will.

When we look at how Isaac's behavior affected Jacob's life, I want you to notice how the principle of sowing and reaping worked in their lives. Remember how Isaac's favorite son was Esau and Rebekah's favorite son was Jacob? Well, Jacob carried on that same behavior; his favorite son was Joseph:

Now Israel [Jacob] *loved Joseph more than all his children . . .* (Genesis 37:3).

129

Favoritism certainly brought heartache to Jacob's entire family. Joseph's brothers were jealous of him because of their father's preferential treatment. They hated Joseph because he had a dream in which he was in authority over them:

And his brethren said to him, Shalt thou indeed reign over us? or shalt thou indeed have dominion over us? And they hated him yet the more for his dreams, and for his words (Genesis 37:8).

Finally, the brothers took Joseph and threw him into a pit. They killed a goat, put its blood on Joseph's special multi-colored coat, took the coat to their father, and told him Joseph had been killed by a wild animal. In reality, they had sold their own brother into slavery (see Genesis 37:28).

Did you notice that Jacob's sons were using a method similar to that which Jacob had used to deceive Isaac—an animal skin? You can sow wrong things in your future too. Jacob sowed some wrong things, and his whole family suffered because he did not walk in godly wisdom.

But Joseph is another success story—he stayed true to God throughout his whole life and became the key to rescuing them during the great famine (see Genesis 45:7). Joseph finally revealed his identity to his family and treated them like kings. Joseph had lived his whole life in faith. He walked in much godly wisdom; and certainly secured the future for his family.

Joseph's life is a wonderful testimony of how we believers can maintain our faith in God's Word. We can walk in godly wisdom even when our circumstances fail us. We can Satan-proof our lives by walking in righteousness and holiness. We can pray that our children will never be conformed to the world but that they will transform it. That's God's wisdom to us. Joseph was a very wise man. He definitely made a difference in the lives of an entire nation.

I believe seeing Joseph walk in godly wisdom really blessed Jacob, whose name by now had been changed to *Israel*, which means "one who prevails with God and man." And when Israel neared the end of his life, he secured his family's future:

And it came to pass after these things, that one told Joseph, Behold, thy father is sick: and he took with him his two sons, Manasseh and Ephraim. . . . And he said, Bring them, I pray thee, unto me, and I will bless them (Genesis 48:1,9).

But when Israel began to pray for his grandsons, he did something very strange:

And Israel stretched out his right hand, and laid it upon Ephraim's head, who was the younger, and his left hand upon Manasseh's head . . . (Genesis 48:14).

Israel began to bless Joseph and said, ". . . *God, before whom my fathers Abraham and Isaac did walk, the God which fed me all my life long unto this day*" (Genesis 48:15). Israel went on to tell Joseph how his seed would be blessed. But Joseph became a little disturbed when he noticed that his father was giving the firstborn blessing to Ephraim instead of Manasseh, who was the oldest (see Genesis 48:17–18). Joseph tried to correct his father, but Israel stood firm in his blessing. And in studying the history of Ephraim, I found that when he got into the Promised Land, his tribe grew so much that the Ephraimites covered the land more than any other tribe. Manasseh wasn't too far behind him, but Ephraim prospered the most. Why? Because Ephraim's future had been secured by Israel, who in his latter years began to walk in faith and in godly wisdom.

Now when Joseph neared his death, I was puzzled by what he said:

And Joseph took an oath of the children of Israel, saying, God will surely visit you, and ye shall carry up my bones from hence (Genesis 50:25).

At one time I was troubled by this strange request, but God showed me that Joseph knew the Israelites were going to be in Egypt for over four hundred years. How? Genesis 15 tells us that Abraham entered into covenant with God, and God said He would deliver Abraham's seed out of Egypt. Abraham shared God's Word with Isaac, Isaac shared God's Word with Jacob, and Jacob shared God's Word with his children. Based on his faith in God and the testimony of God's Word about the Israelites, Joseph had faith for the future of an entire nation. And I want you to know that when the Israelites were delivered from bondage in Egypt, they carried Joseph's bones with them. They carried those bones around in the wilderness for forty years. They didn't have the written Word—but they certainly had the assurance that their future had been secured.

Now let's review the three blessings for your future: material, inheritance, and victory. Just as Abraham blessed Isaac with all his substance, God also wants to bless His people with material blessings. He wants you to be blessed and to prosper. Why? So, you can be a blessing to the kingdom of God. When you sow financial seeds into God's kingdom, you can expect to reap financial blessings in return.

The same thing holds true for prayer. If you will sacrifice time each day for prayer not only for yourself but also for your household, someone will inherit the deposit you are making in your prayer account. And if you sow prayers, you will reap answers in your own life.

Lastly, God wants His people to have faith for future victories. When you begin to Satan-proof your household by walking in faith and in godly wisdom, you will get a clearer understanding of the hope we have in Jesus Christ:

Who shall change our vile body, that it may be fashioned like unto his glorious body, according to the working whereby he is able even to subdue all things unto himself (Philippians 3:21).

If the only hope we had was in this life, then we'd all be miserable people. But if you have been born again, then your hope is not in this life or in this body. The Bible says that Jesus is going to raise our bodies and make them like His! So, despite the circumstances around you, get excited, because through Jesus Christ God has secured the future for all His children throughout eternity.

CHAPTER EIGHT

TURN ON THE LIGHT

Now I want to look at how Satan-proofers can turn on the light wherever there is darkness. You know, at one time every one of us was in darkness:

For ye were sometimes darkness, but now are ye light in the Lord: walk as children of the light (Ephesians 5:8).

In this verse, the apostle Paul was exhorting the Christians not to be partakers of the sinful lifestyle from which they had been delivered. The same holds true for us today. Sometimes we try to measure the depth of the darkness in which we may have been involved. On our rating scale, we consider some types of darkness to be greater than others. Nevertheless, the Word of God warns all of us not to return to the lifestyles we were involved in before we accepted Jesus Christ as our Lord and Savior.

LIGHT REFLECTORS

When you were born again, God destined you to be conformed into the image of Jesus Christ (see Romans 8:29). An image is a reflection—you are being made to be a reflection of Jesus, the Light of the world (see John 3:19; 9:5). You're not the actual Light itself, but you are a Light reflector. Look at the sun and the stars: although they may seem to be the source of light for planet earth, the sun and stars are merely reflectors. The source of light is the same as the source of everything, the Word of God (see Genesis 1:3). The same is true for us; we are people who have been destined to be Satan-proofers by reflecting God's Word and His will on the earth.

I want you to see how you can walk in God's light and change the circumstances around you. You can Satan-proof your circumstances when you allow God's light to shine forth in your relationships with other people.

When Jesus comes into our hearts and we begin to allow ourselves to be conformed into His image, we become instruments God can use to reflect His light—His Word and His will. As we continue to grow in our relationship with the Lord, He will give us more opportunities to reflect His light (Word and will) in the lives of other people. Also, there will be many times when you'll meet people who will turn on the light for you. There may come a time when you will be surrounded by the darkness of uncertainty, or lack of faith. You won't know what to do next about your circumstances, and that's when God will send another believer who will turn on the light for you.

I remember some years ago, we were trying to get a loan for a new church building. It was very difficult because, at that time, Denver banks were not loaning money to churches. The building we had moved from hadn't sold right away; and even if it had, the money would not have been nearly enough to meet this new challenge. We had sort of a rent-to-own agreement on the new building. And, if we couldn't meet our first month's obligation, the cost of the building would go up by $120,000!

This was a very dark time for our ministry. Wally and I were certain that the Lord had led us to acquire a new building, but the finances just didn't seem to be available. Then, one of our church members came up and said, "I believe we can get a loan."

For eight months this man went from bank to bank trying to get financing. When we would ask him about his progress, he would respond, "No, not yet; but we are going to get a loan!" He kept the light turned on for us. And two weeks before the closing, two banks said "yes!" We got the loan the day before we would have had to pay the $120,000 increase!

What helped us to get through this stressful period? One of God's Light reflectors! Our friend was moving in supernatural faith—the faith of Christ—for this situation, and God certainly performed a miracle on our behalf.

How about you? Can you remember a time when you turned on the light through standing in faith and prayer with someone during a time when their situation looked hopeless? Or perhaps you may have been the one who faced a difficult situation that seemed to be beyond your level of faith. Does our loving, heavenly Father leave us alone during those stressful periods? NO! God will send someone to turn on the light—someone to stand on God's Word with you and to pray so His will can be done in your life.

The Bible tells how Seth turned on the light after Abel was killed by their brother Cain. Abel was supposed to be the one who carried the line from Adam and Eve. You could say that, in a sense, Abel was the seed of promise—the light. Can you imagine what would have happened if we all would have been descendants of an ungodly man such as Cain? Thank God that Adam and Eve had another son Seth:

And Adam knew his wife again; and she bare a son, and called his name Seth: For God, said she, hath appointed me another seed instead of Abel, whom Cain slew (Genesis 4:25).

During the time of Seth's son, Enos, men began to call upon the name of the Lord. Why? Because Seth became a light reflector—he was a godly man who had taught his family how to pray, and they turned on the light for the next generation.

Let me tell you, God will never let His light go out! He will always have men and women who He can use to manifest His Word and will on the earth. Satan-proofers are just believers who turn on God's light in every situation in which they become involved.

When I think about a light, I can't help thinking about Noah. He lived during a time when it seemed as though God absolutely had become fed up with everybody! People were involved in all types of sin—the women had even become sexually involved with fallen angels, and the children of these ungodly unions were giants (see Genesis 6:2,4). God was so disgusted by all the terrible things they were doing that He was sorry He had ever created man:

. . . I will destroy man whom I have created from the face of the earth . . . for it repenteth me that I have made them (Genesis 6:7).

Sometimes, I think we get so upset when we think about the terrible conditions in which we live. But let me ask you, when is the last time you saw a giant walking around? Women, you might be experiencing some problems with your unsaved husbands, but at least you aren't married to one of the wicked angels who had been kicked out of heaven along with Satan! Yet, in Noah's day, these things were common.

It's no wonder that God became fed up! And just when it looked as though it could have been curtains for the inhabitants of the earth, Noah found favor with God; and he and his family were spared from destruction:

But Noah found grace in the eyes of the LORD (Genesis 6:8).

Out of the entire human race, only Noah and his family allowed themselves to reflect God's Word and His will. Noah loved God; he led his family in the ways of God; and they certainly turned on God's light during that dark period in history.

When you think about becoming a Satan-proofer—someone who turns on God's light in the world, you might think, "Well, I'm not important. I'm just one person." However, just as one candle can light up a dark room, one believer can light up a dark situation.

You may be the only one in your family who is a reflector of God's wonderful Word and His will. Just hang in there; if you don't turn on the light for your own loved ones, who will? Even if you become discouraged with them or with yourself, remember that God has placed you there to keep His light turned on in their lives.

One of our care group leaders shared that, at one time, he had lived with a woman to whom he was not married. These two had been brought up in the church, but they had turned their backs on the Lord and had begun to live a worldly lifestyle. One day,

God sent a believer who really turned on God's light in that dark situation. The woman was invited to attend one of our services; and while she attended church, her boyfriend stayed home to watch football.

She was born again and Spirit-filled, then she turned on the light in her home. Her boyfriend became born again and Spirit-filled; they were married and now have three beautiful children. They have a wonderful ministry in our care groups, and he recently has entered full-time ministry!

How did this happen? Because one person obeyed God, and God used this believer to turn on His light in this couple's life. I love the way God gets so much mileage out of just one believer who is willing to reflect the light of Jesus in the world.

Someone else who reflected God's light was Joseph. He certainly kept God's light turned on for Israel, as well as for Egypt. The nation of Israel was still a small family at this time—just Israel's (Jacob's) household which was composed of about 70 people. Joseph had been separated from his family because his brothers had become so jealous and evil that they sold him into slavery. Joseph endured terrible hardships and temptations; but Joseph didn't give in to Potiphar's wife, he didn't give in to the pressures of prison, and he didn't give in to bitterness toward his brothers.

No, Joseph stayed true to God; and God gave him a plan to save Egypt and that whole Middle East area during a tremendous famine. Joseph's family survived because he kept God's light burning. If there ever comes a time when you begin to feel unimportant, just remember Joseph and keep turning on God's light wherever you go. There have been so many men like Joseph who allowed themselves to be used by God to turn a particular situation around. Moses was another one. When God spoke to Moses and told him to get the Israelites out of Egypt, at first Moses completely blew it. He did everything all wrong and had to go out in the desert to get some more training. For 40 years Moses cared for his father-in-law, Jethro's, sheep; certainly was an effective training ground for one who would pastor the entire nation of Israel (which had grown to about two million by now).

Finally, God commissioned Moses to go down to Egypt and deal with Pharaoh about releasing the Israelites from slavery. Moses and Aaron obeyed God, and they definitely turned on God's light. Through a series of miracles, God began to deal with Pharaoh. Eventually the people were set free.

PRAYER TURNS ON GOD'S LIGHT

Moses led the Israelites on what turned out to be a 40-year journey through the wilderness. Moses really had plenty of opportunities to turn on God's light for His people. But those people just murmured and complained the whole time they were in the wilderness. So much so, that the entire generation, except for Joshua and Caleb, died in the wilderness without ever getting to cross over into the Promised Land.

I think Moses' life gives us insight as to how God wants believers to respond when our loved ones seem to want to stay in the darkness of sin. One time, when Moses had gone up on Mount Sinai to talk with God, the people became very impatient because Moses had been gone so long. They told Aaron to make them a golden calf. God said to Moses, "I am so disgusted with them I want to wipe the whole crowd out and start over with you" (see Exodus 32:10).

How did Moses respond? He could have said, "Well, God, that's a good idea, because all they do is murmur and whine." But he didn't. Instead, Moses said, "God, if You blot them out, then blot me out too." One man saved the whole nation of Israel. How? By standing in prayer, he turned on God's light for the people.

Just as Moses turned on God's light for the children of Israel through prayer, so can we pray God's light into each other's circumstances. A while back, we were going through a very difficult time with our son. Michael had gotten involved with drugs, and he had begun trying to involve some of the young people of the church in drugs. This was a very dark time for Wally and me. The devil would taunt us saying things like, "Why are you in the ministry? Even your own child isn't serving God. Who are you to get up and preach to the people? What is the church going to say about you? What are people going to say about you?"

Well, Wally and I just told our members the truth. We said, "We're having a hard time. Our son is in trouble, and we're in trouble. Will you please pray for us?" I never heard any criticism. They were absolutely fantastic and said, "We're going to pray for you. We're going to fast for you. And, we're going to hold on to God's Word for you." Our congregation kept the light turned on for us. It's no wonder that we think our church members are so wonderful!

Another one of my favorite light reflectors is Gideon. I know that sometimes we tend to look down on Gideon because when the angel first came to him, Gideon was so pitiful. But the angel

142

saw Gideon in God's image—as a light reflector:

... *The LORD is with thee, thou mighty man of valour* (Judges 6:12).

Gideon's response was something like, "Who me? Do you know about me? I have a low IQ. My family is poor, and we live on the wrong side of the tracks." Gideon's self-esteem was literally in the pits. But the angel didn't pay any heed to Gideon's low opinion of himself. He said, "Gideon, you and God can rid the land of the Midianites" (see Judges 6:16).

Now during this time, it looked like all of Israel was going to be wiped out by the Midianites; and it certainly didn't look like Gideon was capable of doing anything to stop them. Yet Gideon continued to listen to God, and God continued to deal with Gideon. Finally, God sent Gideon out to fight the Midianites with only 300 men. You say, "300 men against a whole army! They must have had some very powerful weapons."

You'll be surprised to know that they only had four types of weapons: trumpets, pitchers, lamps, and swords (see Judges 7:16). They blew the trumpets, took the sword, hit the pitcher, and the light sprang forth as they shouted, "The sword of the Lord and of Gideon!" This little band of soldiers absolutely defeated the fierce Midianite army. How? By carrying God's light.

How often do we allow opportunities to turn on God's light to slip away because we are afraid? Some of you look at yourselves and say, "Well, I've never attended Bible school. I didn't graduate from high school. I don't have any experience. I'm not good looking. I've got a big nose. I say the wrong things. Or, I just can't do it!" But those are all lies from the devil because you can do all things through Christ, Who strengthens you (see Philippians 4:13). Despite your shortcomings and faults, God can use you to turn on His light in the circumstances around you. Look at all the men I have mentioned. They all had faults, but they were willing to listen to God; and as they began to respond to God, He used them to turn their situations around.

It's a tremendous blessing when God allows you to turn on the light in a dark situation. It's also a blessing when God sends someone to turn on the light for you. One time, many years ago, I felt like some of my staff were just going to quit the ministry because they may have thought I had made some wrong decisions. One young woman came to me crying; I thought she had come to quit. So, I asked, "Are you going to quit?" She said, "Quit? No! God called me here; and although I may not understand everything you do, I have confidence in you." Her encouragement meant so much to me. It was as if she had turned the light back on for me.

I want you to know that you won't always be aware when you have turned on the light for someone. That's why we must be so cautious to be led by the Holy Spirit in our dealings with people. Sometimes God's loving light may shine through someone's darkness because of your smile, prayers, or kind words. Turning on God's light doesn't always have to be through some big thing. For the most part, God's light will shine in the little things that we do.

I read an interesting description about a glowworm. The steps it takes are so small, they can hardly be measured. And as the glowworm moves across a field at midnight, it produces just enough light in its glow to illuminate one single step forward. So as the glowworm moves ahead, it always moves into light.

Sometimes God will allow you to bless others in a way which will produce very obvious results in their lives. But, usually God will allow you to be like the glowworm. You'll turn God's light on during someone's dark moments or moods, and little by little they will begin to move into God's direction for their lives.

AN UNEXPECTED LIGHT REFLECTOR

You know, sometimes God's light may be turned on by the most unexpected people; such as the child, Samuel. He came on the scene during a very pitiful situation. Samuel probably expected Eli to be the one who would turn on the light. After all, Eli was the high priest who was supposed to instruct Samuel in the priesthood. But, sadly, Eli was not obedient to God's instructions concerning child-rearing. Eli had two sons, Hophni and Phinehas, whom he had so indulged that he hadn't disciplined or trained them. They were involved in adultery, and were stealing from the sacrifices (see 1 Samuel 2:12–16,22).

It certainly looked like God's light for Israel's spiritual atmosphere was about to go out. However, instead of Eli turning on the light for Israel, Samuel was God's man for the occasion.

Even as a young boy, God had begun to talk to Samuel and Samuel had begun to listen to God's voice (see 1 Samuel 3:4–14). Samuel didn't become rebellious toward Eli and say, "You're a poor example to me. How can I be a believer? And look at your kids; they're the pits." No, Samuel kept holding on to God's Word.

Later when Israel was attacked by the Philistines (see 1 Samuel

4:1), the Ark of God was taken and both of Eli's sons were killed in battle. When Eli heard the news:

. . . he fell from off the seat backward by the side of the gate, and his neck brake, and he died: for he was an old man, and heavy. And he had judged Israel forty years (1 Samuel 4:18).

And there is something else that happened to Eli's son, Phinehas', wife, who was pregnant and went into labor when the news came. Evidently, she was not in good health because when her son was born, she was near death (see 1 Samuel 4:20). She completely ignored her son:

And she named the child Ichabod, saying, The glory is departed from Israel . . . (1 Samuel 4:21).

She thought God's light had been turned off, but she was wrong. The glory of God hadn't departed from Israel. Do you know why? Because Samuel had God's light on the inside of him.

It doesn't matter who blows it or backslides; that is not our problem. A Satan-proofer will keep God's light on. Jesus is the Light, and He is inside every believer. If we will stand in His light, who knows what we can do for those who backslide or blow it!

A woman called in one day with a praise report. Previously she had requested prayer because her son's girlfriend was pregnant and was scheduled to have an abortion. However, a Christian friend began to pray with the girl and helped her to understand that abortion was wrong. Praise God, the girlfriend changed her mind and decided to keep her baby.

I don't know whether this girl has received Christ or not; but I do know that her Christian friend turned on God's light in this dark situation.

Folks, when we pray for each other, we are turning on God's light. I love to turn on God's light for other people. Don't you? Wouldn't you rather pray and bring forth God's Word and His will in people's lives than to turn God's light off by participating in gossip and strife? Well, evidently Samuel chose to keep the light on for Israel; and the nation didn't go under because God's light shined through Samuel.

When I travel, sometimes people come to me with all kinds of stories about troublesome leadership in their churches. I always challenge them to be Satan-proofers. I ask, "Well, are you standing in faith? Are you praying? Or, are you criticizing and being negative?" Sometimes I think that God allows us to see problems so we can pray and keep the light turned on until He turns the situation around. Another place I have seen people turn on God's light is for marriages that look like they are falling apart. One mate will keep God's light burning, and many of those marriages are standing strong today. Why? Because one believing mate refuses to let God's light go out for his or her marriage.

There was another time in Israel's history when it looked like the light of God's spiritual atmosphere was about to go out. A king named Jehoram had married a wicked woman named Athaliah—she is absolutely the worst woman in the Bible. You may be thinking, "No, Jezebel is the worst." Well, Athaliah was Jezebel's daughter; and I think Athaliah was much better at being evil than Jezebel.

After Athaliah's husband died, their son Ahaziah took the throne of Judah and was killed while visiting the king of Israel. Athaliah wanted the throne so much that she ordered the murder of her own grandchildren (see 2 Kings 11:1). This woman certainly was the pits! Her actions could have eliminated all hope for the Messiah to come forth from the house of David. This would have been absolutely devastating for Israel and for you and me (the Body of Christ) as well!

But God had a provision for this critical situation. God's provision came in the form of a priest named Jehoiada, who had married Athaliah's daughter Jehosheba. When her mother began to murder all the children, Jehosheba slipped in, took the only remaining grandchild, Joash, and hid him from his wicked grandmother (see 2 Kings 11:2). I really admire Jehosheba's courage and her desire to do God's will, even though it meant going against her mother, who was quite capable of killing Jehosheba in the process.

But Jehosheba probably said something like, "God will take care of me. If I perish, I perish; but the light cannot go out for the house of David." So, she stole that little tiny baby and hid him in her home for six years. She and Jehoiada raised Joash; and when he was seven years old, they secretly took him into the Temple to be crowned the rightful king of Israel:

And when Athaliah heard the noise of the guard and of the people, she came to the people into the temple of the LORD (2 Kings 11:13).

In the midst of the celebration, Athaliah came running down the aisle crying, "Treason, treason."

And they laid hands on her; and she went by the way by the which the horses came into the king's house: and there was she slain (2 Kings 11:16).

Despite all the devil's attempts, God's light will never go out! He will always have men and women—Satan-proofers—who will say, "God, I am going to stay true to You and turn Your light on in this situation."

I'll give you another example of someone who reflected God's will, Daniel. While Daniel was enslaved in Babylon, he turned on God's light for three kings: Nebuchadnezzar, Belshazzar, and Darius. Daniel had favor with God in the area of interpreting dreams and visions. Now Daniel could have sold out and turned away from God's people; after all, they had been taken into captivity because of their own sin. But Daniel stayed true to God and to God's people, and he prayed for the Jews.

Then one night something very strange happened while King Belshazzar was having a big drunken brawl:

In the same hour came forth fingers of a man's hand, and wrote . . . upon the plaister of the wall of the king's palace . . . (Daniel 5:5).

Can you imagine how unusual that must have been? Suddenly a hand appeared out of nowhere and began to write on the wall. Well, Belshazzar was simply terrified:

Then the king's countenance was changed, and his thoughts troubled him, so that the joints of his loins were loosed, and his knees smote one against another (Daniel 5:6).

I think it's almost funny! Here Belshazzar was making a mockery out of God by allowing the golden vessels that were taken out of the Temple to be used as drinking containers at this party. But what happened when the hand of God appeared? Belshazzar's face became pale, his whole body began to tremble, and his knees started knocking!

None of the king's astrologers or soothsayers knew what had been written. In fact, there was only one person in the entire kingdom who could interpret the handwriting on the wall. That's right—Daniel was the only man who could turn on God's light for that situation. When you look around you and see all the trouble in the world, don't get nervous because it can't be that dark if you're around. You are a Satan-proofer—God's provision for the situation. All you have to do is to turn on God's light wherever you go.

The last person I want to tell you about is Saul (Paul):

And as he journeyed, he came near Damascus: and suddenly there shined round about him a light from heaven (Acts 9:3).

Before Saul met Jesus, he was in darkness. Even though he may have loved God, he was trying to serve God with his mind and his legalistic teaching. However, God wanted Paul to turn on His light and so God sent the Light—Jesus—to Paul. After Paul had received the Light of Christ, God made him a light to the Gentiles (see Acts 13:47). God sent Paul to preach to the Gentiles, and that was the beginning of a tremendous revival which would extend all the way down to you and me.

I want to tell you that just as Paul was a Light reflector, you and I are Light reflectors too. Jesus is the Light of the world; and although we believers are not the actual Light itself, we reflect the Word and the will of the marvelous Light Who dwells inside us. Through the power of God, we can be Satan-proofers as we reflect God's Word and His will throughout the earth.

CHAPTER NINE

GETTING GOD'S PRIORITIES

If I were to ask you what you thought God's number one priority is, would you answer, "People?" If so, you'd be exactly right. God is just wild over people! We are His number one priority. The Bible says:

And God blessed them, and God said unto them, Be fruitful, and multiply, and replenish the earth . . . (Genesis 1:28).

This scripture lets us know that God loved people so much that He wasn't satisfied with just one couple, He wanted the earth to be inhabited with lots and lots of people. So, He told Adam and Eve, "I want you to go forth and bring forth fruit—have children—and replenish the earth." Notice how God refers to people as "fruit." I guess we could say that God's favorite fruit is children:

Lo, children are an heritage of the LORD: and the fruit of the womb is his reward (Psalm 127:3).

Here again we see the great importance God places upon children. Those of you who don't yet have children may ask, "How does this teaching apply to me?" It applies to you, because someday, if you get married and have children, you'll need to know how to Satan-proof your children through proper parenting. I believe that if you begin to pray ahead and learn now, God will give you so much wisdom about parenting that by the time you do have children, you'll be absolutely the best parent in the world!

God says children are our heritage—our fruit—our reward. I imagine there are plenty of times when some parents probably feel like they could have done without some of their reward. Nevertheless, God says children are our heritage, God puts a priority on the family, and He considers our children to be extremely important.

GOD'S FIRSTFRUITS

I want to talk to you about firstfruits. When you see the word "firstfruits" in the Bible, it identifies God's priorities. Needless to say, God's firstfruits—priorities—may not always be ours (even though they should be). What are God's firstfruits?

God told the Israelites that their firstfruits—their firstborn male children—belonged to Him. However, instead of literally taking their babies away from them, God designated the entire tribe of Levites to symbolize the firstfruits of the nation of Israel:

And thou shalt take the Levites for me (I am the LORD) instead of all the firstborn among the children of Israel . . . (Numbers 3:41).

The Israelites participated in a dedication ceremony for their children, and on the thirtieth day after the first male child was born, the mother and the father presented their baby to the priest. The priest would ask the mother, "Is this your first-born son?" She would say, "Yes, it is." Then the priest would ask the father, "Is this your firstborn son?" and the father would respond, "Yes, it is." By affirming the child to be their firstborn, these parents symbolically gave the child to God.

Then the parents were required to redeem their child—buy him back—by paying the priest five shekels (about $3.20). (See Numbers 3:40–50.) You may think it pretty strange that they had to buy back their own child—and for only $3.20! Actually, this was a tax that God had imposed to help support the priests and Levites.

However, the concept of redemption is extremely important to you and me today because believers have been redeemed (see Galatians 3:13). We have not been redeemed with corruptible things like silver and gold, but with the precious blood of Jesus (see 1 Peter 1:18; Revelation 5:9). Since God has destined for all people to come into His family, every person born on this earth is a potential firstborn child of God. Do you see how people are God's number one priority?

People aren't God's only firstfruits. God also talked to the Israelites about the firstfruits of their harvest (see Exodus 23:16). God said, "Make Me your priority. Put Me first in whatever you do. At the beginning of the harvest, bring Me your firstfruits." Today, you give God the firstfruits of your harvests when you pay your tithes—ten percent of your pretax income—to the storehouse (your local church). You are saying, "God, You are the priority in my life. You are my source, and I am returning my firstfruits to You."

I received a testimony from a man who said he had been delivered from debt and decrease. He had been employed with an oil company; and although his annual income was just under $50,000, he acquired a $340,000 debt! Then he went through a divorce, changed jobs, and ended up making less than $24,000 per year. Needless to say, he could not pay off the large amount of money he owed. But something else happened to him that year. He rededicated his life to the Lord, became Spirit-filled, and began to learn about tithing. His letter said:

"I am absolutely convinced that if you do not tithe, the devourer is not going to be rebuked. However, if you do tithe, I don't care how big your bills are . . . what God does is to give you favor with your creditors, and that's something I've learned to claim."

This man didn't know how God was going to set him free of financial bondage, but he was determined to tithe despite how futile his financial situation appeared.

Then he said that God began to speak to his heart about giving offerings of $150 to $500 above his normal tithe. At one point, he began to question whether or not he really was hearing from God; he wondered if his mind was playing tricks on him. However, each time He obeyed God in the area of giving, God would supernaturally bless him. By the next year, his debt had been reduced to $250,000 and God said, "I'm going to heal your finances." This man is seeing evidence of this promise more and more each day.

God has commanded His people to tithe:

Bring ye all the tithes into the storehouse . . . (Malachi 3:10).

It's too bad that many Christians allow God to deliver them from all sorts of sinful lifestyles—they attend church regularly and they study their Bibles—but they are not committed tithers. Then they wonder why they never seem to be able to accomplish their financial goals. It's because they do not trust God to Satan-proof their finances by tithing their firstfruits:

And I will rebuke the devourer for your sakes, and he shall not destroy the fruits of your ground . . . (Malachi 3:11)

I have noticed that people who faithfully pay their tithes seem to have much more than people who don't. I have heard some amazing testimonies of how God has taken 90 percent of someone's income and stretched it to meet all financial needs, with some left over. When Christians share their financial problems with me, I always ask, "Do you tithe?" Some people respond, "No, I can't afford it." I tell them, "You really can't afford not to tithe."

Folks, whether we like it or not, we have to obey God; and He said that our tithes—firstfruits—belong to Him. When we give God our firstfruits, it's as if we are planting a seed. God will multiply that seed and bring forth a great harvest.

Another one of God's firstfruits is the nation of Israel:

Israel was holiness unto the LORD, and the firstfruits of his increase: all that devour him shall offend; evil shall come upon them, saith the LORD (Jeremiah 2:3).

God claimed the whole nation of Israel as His; and whenever God talks about His "firsts," He is planning on a big harvest. So, although Israel may have been God's first nation, look at the millions of people from other nations who became born again because of God's dealings with the Israelites.

Israel was the seed from which God expected a great harvest

of many other nations to become His people. The same principle will work for us today concerning our children. When we dedicate our children to God as infants and bring them up in the fear and admonition of God, what happens? God becomes their priority, and they will begin to witness to others about the love of Jesus Christ. They will begin to turn on God's light in people's lives, and this will cause others to come to Christ.

Have you ever heard people say, "You can't outgive God?" That certainly is true; and we can see this when God said, "Because people are my priority and I am asking them to give to Me their firstfruits, I am going to give back to them My best—My firstborn Son." Who is God's firstborn Son? Yes, it's Jesus:

For whom he did foreknow, he also did predestinate to be conformed to the image of his Son, that he might be the firstborn among many brethren (Romans 8:29).

In whom we have redemption through his blood, even the forgiveness of sins: Who is the image of the invisible God, the firstborn of every creature (Colossians 1:14–15).

And again, when he bringeth in the firstbegotten into the world, he saith, And let all the angels of God worship him (Hebrews 1:6).

God gave us His firstborn, Jesus, because He wanted a harvest—a great big family of firstborns. He wanted us all to come into His kingdom and be firstborns too. God's number one priority is people. We have always been God's first concern.

CARING FOR GOD'S PRIORITIES

When we look at how God taught the Israelites to take care of their children, we'll see the image of what kind of parents God wants us to be and how He wants our children to be priorities.

Remember, in Chapter 5 we saw that all people are destined—set apart—to subdue the earth and to be blessed—to be put in an attitude of worship. This can only take place after our minds have been renewed, and we have been conformed into the image of Jesus Christ. Right? Therefore, it's when we become born again that we become God's firstborn.

I really want you to understand that you must be born again. Just because your parents may be born-again Christians does not automatically mean that you are a Christian. No, you have to receive Christ into your life. Your parents may stand in faith for your salvation, but you personally have to be born again.

When you become born again, you become a firstborn because Jesus is God's firstborn—you come into God's family through your faith in Christ. Now look at what Jesus says about you:

And I have declared unto them thy name, and will declare it: that the love wherewith thou hast loved me may be in them, and I in them (John 17:26).

Jesus said that His Heavenly Father loves you just as much as He loves Jesus. I know it may sound too wonderful to be true; nonetheless, God loves you just as much as He loves Jesus.

PROTECTING GOD'S PRIORITIES

Let's look back and see what God said about the Egyptians' firstborn: "I'm going to judge Egypt. I am going to send the devourer and take the firstborn child, and firstborn of every animal in Egypt" (See Exodus 11:4–8, 12:29–30). He had already destroyed the first part of their harvest.

It must have been truly devastating for the Egyptians to have all their firstborn children, animals, and possessions destroyed. They probably wondered why the Israelites weren't experiencing the same catastrophes. The Israelites were under God's protection and obeyed God's Word: "Put the blood of the lamb on your doorposts; then when the death angel passes over, he'll see the blood and your firstborn will be protected because they are under the blood covenant" (see Exodus 12).

God wanted to save the adult Israelites from destruction, but He also wanted to save their children. The same thing holds true today. It's not enough for just you and me (adults) to be saved; God wants our children to be under His blood covenant and become His firstborn through Jesus Christ. Children are our fruit, our reward, our heritage, and it is extremely important to God that our children are born into His kingdom. That's why God told the Israelites to put the blood on the doorposts so their children could become part of their covenant relationship with God.

Now you may be saying, "Yes, Marilyn, but you just said that parents can't make the decision concerning salvation for their children." You're right; however, let me show you what parents can do.

After our relationship with God and our relationship with our spouses, we can make children our first priority. While children are living in our homes, they come under our protective covenant with God:

For the unbelieving husband is sanctified by the wife, and the unbelieving wife is sanctified by the husband: else were your children unclean; but now are they holy (1 Corinthians 7:14).

Did you realize that one believer in the household causes the blood of Jesus to be over that entire household? That's right! The blood of Jesus in one believer sanctifies the home and marks—sets apart or calls God's attention to—everyone living in that household. God not only is interested in that believer, He also wants to establish a covenant relationship with every member of the family. God wants us, as Christian parents, to bring forth our fruit (children) so they can replenish the earth.

Let's compare scripture with scripture and see what Jesus said about your fruit:

. . . and [I have] *ordained you, that ye should go and bring forth fruit, and that your fruit should remain . . .* (John 15:16, emphasis added).

Now look back to Genesis 1:28 where God told Adam and Eve to be fruitful. Then turn to Psalm 127:3–5 which says that children are your fruit because they are your inheritance and your reward. When you bring forth children into the world—and then into God's kingdom—they can be blessed (brought into an attitude of worship). Then they will begin to Satan-proof the earth by becoming Light reflectors. They will reflect God's wonderful Word and His will into the dark places in other people's lives and cause them to come closer to God.

That's why God doesn't want us parents to be so nonchalant when it comes to taking care of our children. We can't just casually give them a Bible and tell them to read it when they get older—if they feel like it! We can't treat our children like that and expect them to be the fruit that remains. God doesn't want our children or grandchildren to be lost; He wants us to take our fruit to heaven with us. And since our children are a number one priority with God, we parents need to be sure our children are a number one priority for us too.

GODLY PRIORITIES vs. WORLDLY PRIORITIES

There is so much emphasis on materialism today. It's no wonder that we refer to the fast pace of today's culture as the "rat race." Some of you have become so involved with keeping up and getting ahead that you actually have begun to neglect your children. For instance, you who need two cars because both parents work, may end up working so hard that you don't have any time to spend with your children. So, what do you do? You go into more debt and purchase a big television set, and you may buy a video game set. Then you worry about the high level of violence that your children are exposed to.

I am not telling you not to work, but many of you have set your priorities in the wrong direction. You may work yourselves to the point where you come home feeling so tired that you do not have time for your children. You try to squeeze all your children's time needs into a tight, little box that we popularly refer to as "quality time." And, sadly, your children are going down the drain because they receive such a low priority in your life. Yet, God says our children are our reward, heritage, and fruit. They are fruit that is to remain after we leave.

I received a testimony from a woman whose father's distorted sense of priorities caused tremendous suffering for his entire family. This man was unable to find employment; and, instead of seeking God's provision for his family, he made a very unwise decision to become involved in organized crime. How tragic! Instead of protecting (Satan-proofing) his family, the man actually became the tool through which Satan brought terrible humiliation and torment to his entire family.

The father's priorities were out of order. Remember, next to our relationship with God and then with our spouses, our children come first. If this father had been seeking God's wisdom for himself first and then his family, this tragedy never would have occurred.

Let's talk about some other wrong priorities, such as cars, houses, or jobs. Again, I am not saying that it is wrong to desire these things, but some of you parents—especially you fathers—may be placing more emphasis on paying for that new car than you do on your children. However, when Jesus returns to rapture the Body of Christ, are you going to say, "Don't forget to take my Cadillac?" You may say it; but, believe me, your car will never make it! Somebody else will be driving it, and you'll have gone to heaven. What about your new house? So, what if it does have five bedrooms and four baths. If you are a believer, after Jesus comes, someone else will be enjoying your house and you'll be gone. And perhaps you have a prestigious position you think very highly of—maybe you're even the president of a company. You can't take your position to heaven with you, but you can take your children with you. Next to God and your spouse, they are the most precious part of your life. They are a number one priority with God, and they need to be a number one priority with you too.

There are four important principles I want to share about taking your children to heaven with you: how to view, teach, pray, and be a role model for them.

HOW DO YOU SEE YOUR CHILDREN?

Some of you may be thinking, "Marilyn, I'd like to take my children with me to heaven. I've tried, but they are just not responding." Regardless of what the circumstances may look like, your children CAN go with you. The first thing to do is learn to see your children as God sees them—precious and valuable. Begin to think of your children as beautiful fruit and prepare them to carry the love of Christ.

Let me share with you a testimony about a young man whose family did not understand that he was a number one priority with God. At a very young age, this boy had been sexually abused by his grandmother and mentally and physically abused by his parents.

After his parents' divorce, the mother began to work, and the boy became a latchkey kid. The mother wrote that her son had been so deeply wounded by all the abuse he had suffered that he tried everything he knew to not be a burden upon her. He took care of the house while his mother worked, he was never late for school, and he was never in any trouble. He lived silently within himself to a point where he never shared with his mother his needs concerning school or anything else. This mother did not see her son as a priority; instead, she focused all her attention on herself and her responsibilities as a single parent.

This family may have ignored their fruit, but the devil certainly didn't. By the time the boy was in the sixth grade, he began to change and started drinking, smoking, and taking drugs. However, his mother's life had begun to change as well. She remarried a man who also became a negative force in her son's life, but she also rededicated herself to God and became Spirit-filled.

The mother began praying for her child, and God began to reveal how the abusive behavior had helped to shape his life. The Holy Spirit instructed her how to be loving, supportive, and understanding—to become the protector of her fruit—even when it meant taking a stand against the abusive behavior of her new husband. She wrote:

"One gift that God has given me is the steadfast determination to follow through once I know I have heard from Him. I have watched my son go from being unloved, abused, and having a terrible chip on his shoulder, to becoming softened and opened to me again. His 'I love ya, Mom,' is more precious than anything else I have ever accomplished with God's help."

Although this family's circumstances may be far from ideal, God is definitely moving in a powerful way to bring forth His desires in the mother and in one of His number one priorities—the child.

Oftentimes when our children are sweet, we think, "Oh, they are a beautiful reward." However, in cases where our children aren't so sweet, we say, "I can't deal with them; they're too hard to handle." Yet, God didn't say our children are our reward only when they were well behaved and nice, did He? No, He said they are our reward, period! No matter how they act, our children are still our inheritance.

It's so important for us to understand that even when we may have blown it with our children and they become difficult to deal with, our children are still our fruit. When we parents begin to trust God and line our lives up with God's Word and His will, pretty soon we'll begin to see our children become the precious and valuable fruit that God sees when He looks at them.

TEACH YOUR CHILDREN

Another thing we Christian parents need to do is to teach God's Word and His principles to our children. Some of you think that bringing your children to Sunday School once a week is enough. But, 45 minutes or an hour per week simply is not enough time for your children to spend learning about God.

The book of Deuteronomy contains the most intense teaching program for children I have ever seen:

And ye shall teach them [God's Words] *your children, speaking of them when thou sittest in thine house, and when thou walkest by the way, when thou liest down, and when thou risest up. And thou shalt write them upon the door posts of thine house, and upon thy gates: That your days may be multiplied, and the days of your children, in the land which the LORD sware unto your fathers to give them, as the days of heaven upon the earth* (Deuteronomy 11:19–21).

God puts the responsibility for our children learning about Him squarely upon our shoulders! Let me ask you, do you read the Bible with your children? Do you share how God's Word applies to their everyday situations? If you want to please God concerning your children, then give Him reason to say of you as He said of Abraham:

For I know him, that he will command his children and his household after him, and they shall keep the way of the LORD . . . (Genesis 18:19).

Christians are the seed of Abraham. What did God say about Abraham's seed? He said, *"That in blessing I will bless thee, and in multiplying I will multiply thy seed"* (Genesis 22:17). Friends, God wants to bless and multiply us, and He wants to bless and multiply our seed. But like Abraham, we must understand that this blessing won't happen automatically just because our children were born into our households. No, your children will be blessed and multiplied when you do your part and teach them in the ways of the Lord.

Begin to Satan-proof your children by applying the blood of Jesus to their lives, seeing them as valuable individuals, and teaching them God's Word. Then when they are old enough, they will make the same wise decision to receive our loving Savior into their hearts as you did.

When my son, Mike, was about ten or eleven years old, I began to memorize the book of Proverbs. I thought it would be good if my children memorized some of it too, so I had Mike and Sarah memorize the first six chapters of Proverbs.

One day, Mike said, "Mother, I have talked with the kids at church, and you're the only mother who makes her children memorize Proverbs." I didn't respond, so he became more dramatic, "You know, Mother, you're probably the only mother in the whole city who makes your children memorize Proverbs." When

I still didn't respond, Mike became a little desperate, "Mother! This is horrible; you're the only mother in the whole wide world who makes her child memorize Proverbs!" I said, "I think that's wonderful, Mike. You are so blessed to have the only mother in the world who is helping you to memorize God's Word."

The Bible says if we raise up our children in the ways of God, when they are old, they will not depart from our teaching (see Proverbs 22:6). When you begin to plant God's Word into your children, remember that the Word cannot return void. God's Word will always prosper and accomplish the work that God has set forth in your children's lives.

PRAYING DAILY FOR YOUR CHILDREN

The third important point is daily prayer. Wally and I always supported our children in their school activities. One day, at one of Sarah's basketball games, the woman sitting next to me shared that she and her husband were born again and Spirit-filled. However, when they shared the good news of their conversion with their two teenage daughters, the daughters became very upset. They began to gripe and complain because their parents prayed and quoted scriptures at meal times. The daughters would say, "We're so tired of all this 'Amen' and 'Hallelujah' stuff!" The girls really were resistant to their parents' new lifestyle, and there was a lot of strife within the home.

So, the woman began to pray and ask God to give her wisdom in this situation. The Lord told her to fast one day a week and pray for her children, and she did that for seven months. Now both of her daughters are born again and Spirit-filled, and they join their mother and father in praising the Lord.

Pray for your children on a regular basis, and don't forget to pray with them. Many times, I hear parents talk about how much time they spend praying for their children, but they neglect to pray with them. Along with teaching our children the Word of God, we need to teach them how to pray fervently:

. . . The effectual fervent prayer of a righteous man availeth much (James 5:16).

That word *fervent* can mean "heated to the welding point." Make sure that your children know how to pray those white-hot prayers that really get things moving in the spirit realm.

Let's look at another thing about prayer. One morning I was praying for my son, and the Lord spoke to my heart, "Marilyn, you're going to get your reward in your children." When I asked God how this would happen, He impressed upon me:

. . . for he that cometh to God must believe that he is, and that he is a rewarder of them that diligently seek him (Hebrews 11:6).

When we diligently seek God concerning our children, we will see our children as our reward. So, start praying right now for your children. Pray for their education, friends, and mates. Start Satan-proofing their future. In the name of Jesus, claim that your children are going to heaven with you—even if you have to drag them by their heels!

Begin a daily vigil over your children. Rebuke the devil and in Jesus' name refuse to let him have your seed! Determine within yourself that you are going to pray your children in; and even if it happens the last second before they die, they will receive Jesus into their heart.

LIVING HOLY LIVES BEFORE YOUR CHILDREN

Lastly, I want to talk about your lifestyle. You simply cannot live a double standard before your children. You can't tell your children, "I don't want you to drink, smoke, take drugs, or become sexually active," unless you are living a clean life yourself. They'll think of you as a hypocrite, and they'll be right. If you live a sloppy life, then you can't expect your children to prosper because you're sowing bad seed into their lives.

One woman told me that she really wanted her daughter to be born again and to commit herself totally to Jesus Christ. Now this mother was a Christian, but she was haphazard in her church attendance and she didn't tithe. I'm going to tell you something: your children will reap the type of life that you sow. Your children will follow your example.

The Bible says that one believer sanctifies the family. If you're not conducting your life according to God's Word, then don't expect your children to live a consecrated life either.

Before we go any further, I would like for you to pray with me:

Dear heavenly Father, I thank You today for Your wonderful Word and the assurance for my children. Thank You for my rewards, my inheritance, and for this marvelous fruit which You have put in my hands. Now, Father, I lift up those areas where I have failed and I repent. From now on, after my relationship with You and my spouse, I commit my children to be my number one priority. I promise to view them as valuable individuals, to teach them Your Word (if I cannot share personally, I will mail Your Word to them), to pray for them, and to lead a holy life before them. In Jesus' name, when I go to heaven I know my children will be following me. Amen.

CHAPTER TEN

TRANSFORMING POWER

I am sure that you all want to see your families go forward; you want to see your spouses, children, and the rest of your loved ones really begin to walk victoriously in the Lord. So, when your loved ones are suffering, wounded, or defeated, it hurts you too, doesn't it?

I remember the first time my daughter Sarah had a high temperature. She was only about three months old, and we were planning a trip to Nebraska. She was so sick. We prayed and prayed, but she didn't seem to get any better—in fact, she got worse. Finally, Wally said, "I'm going to go to the drugstore to get something for her. Call the doctor; we just can't go on like this."

To see our helpless little baby suffering was so difficult for us. I know that most of you have (or will) feel the same way. It hurts to see your loved ones suffer. It also hurts us when we know our loved ones are not walking in the victory available for them in Jesus Christ. However, as Satan-proofers we are not going to focus upon the hurts; we are going to focus on Jesus Christ! By faith, we are going to take authority over their situations and begin to operate in God's transforming power for our loved ones. That is the purpose of a Satan-proofer—to transform the circumstances around you (subdue the earth).

God never intended for us to sit passively by and watch the devil cover the earth with destruction. That's why God gave believers authority over the devil:

Behold, I give unto you power to tread on serpents and scorpions, and over all the power of the enemy: and nothing shall by any means hurt you (Luke 10:19).

In Chapter Six we saw that the first time the word *power* appears in this verse refers to "authority" and the second time the word *power* appears refers to "miracle-working power." You received God's authority the moment you were born again. And if you have been baptized in the Holy Spirit, you have been given God's miracle-working power. What are you supposed to do with God's authority and power? Stop Satan from wreaking havoc in the area where you have influence.

There was a woman from Chicago, who had been participating in our Bible reading plan. She wrote that her son had been classified by the police as a habitual criminal—he was hopelessly locked into a criminal mindset. But praise God, as she began to feed herself with God's Word, it began to change her from being hopeless to hopeful about her son:

Though hand join in hand, the wicked shall not be unpunished: but the seed of the righteous shall be delivered (Proverbs 11:21).

This woman had gotten ahold of God's Word concerning a promise for her son. She began to Satan-proof her child and reminded God of His Word, "Father, You promised me that my seed will be delivered." Let me tell you, God's Word is transforming power and it absolutely reversed the course of her son's life.

This diligent mother stood on Proverbs 11:21. She began to meditate on it, she spoke it out loud, and she prayed it. During the testimony service at her church, she boldly proclaimed, "I know God is going to save my son, and he will preach the gospel in this church."

Of course, the other members thought, "You poor, deluded woman. Your son is always going to be the pits." Yet, she said, "Marilyn, I didn't let the dirty looks affect me. I just held onto God's Word." She had focused all her attention on God's Word—His transforming power.

One night at ten o'clock, she felt an unusual burden to pray for her son in tongues. He called her (long distance) an hour later, asking what she had been doing between 10:00 and 10:30 that night. He had sold some bad drugs to a man who had come to his apartment during that time, and the man had beat him to a pulp. The man pulled out a gun intending to shoot my friend's son but whenever he tried to pull the trigger, his finger would not bend! He tried several times, but he just couldn't do it. Finally, he threw the gun down and ran out saying, "Your mother is doing something to stop me from pulling this trigger!" Imagine, this gunman knew that his intended victim's mother was stopping him from killing her son!

She had been praying God's Word for her son—God's trans-forming power. When the son came home, he was born again, Spirit-filled, attended Bible school, and was invited to be the guest speaker at their church.

You see, your loved ones can be transformed! If they are living a life that is filled with hopelessness and despair, then it's because they are living outside of God's will. God's will is His Word; it is His transforming power; and it can have tremendous consequences in your life as well as in the lives of your loved ones.

I am going to give you five things to consider as you begin to Satan-proof your household through God's transforming power: the father's faith; it's time for our loved ones to arise; the mother's faith; power to transform the past; and catching the faith vision for your loved ones.

THE FATHER'S FAITH

We're going to look first at the faith of fathers:

So Jesus came again into Cana of Galilee, where he made the water wine. And there was a certain nobleman, whose son was sick at Capernaum (John 4:46).

This man was a Gentile and was very prosperous. This man's son was very, very ill; no one expected the child to live. Although the nobleman was not a believer, he was so moved by compassion for his son that he found Jesus and asked Him to heal the boy. Jesus didn't respond favorably to his first plea and called the man a sign-seeker. But when the nobleman asked Him again, Jesus responded:

. . . Go thy way; thy son liveth . . . (John 4:50).

This child had a problem; he was almost dying—and this father took his son to Jesus—not physically, but by faith. What are you fathers supposed to do when your children have problems? Do you become nervous, start biting your nails, and pulling out your hair? No! Do you say, "Oh, I'm letting my wife handle our children?" No!

174

What happened when that nobleman took his son, by faith, to Jesus? Jesus spoke the Word, which is God's transforming power, and the boy was miraculously healed. And not only was the child healed, the whole family was born again! The transforming power of Jesus Christ always does more than we can ask or think. All we need do is to get ahold of God's Word and begin to apply it to our circumstances.

Just hearing Jesus speak the Word increased the nobleman's faith so much that, instead of running home to see if his son had been healed, the man went about his business and didn't go home until the next day. He had gotten ahold of God's Word— His transforming power—and the man's faith skyrocketed right into the supernatural.

So then faith cometh by hearing, and hearing by the word of God (Romans 10:17).

When the nobleman finally did go home, his servants rushed out to meet him. They said, "Guess what happened? Your son is healed!" The man asked the servants to pinpoint the exact hour that his son began to recover. They told him, and it was the same hour Jesus had spoken the words of healing. And, you know, just as God's transforming power worked in this family, it will work for your family today!

You may think, "Well, my children aren't sick." But perhaps you suspect your son or daughter of being involved in drugs, alcohol, or illicit sex. Or, maybe you have evidence that your children have become involved in the occult. You say, "I've talked to them and done everything I can think of, but my children won't listen to me." Hang on, and listen to how one man dealt with a similar problem:

. . . there came to him [Jesus] *a certain man, kneeling down to him,* [Jesus] *and saying, Lord, have mercy on my son: for he is lunatick, and sore vexed: for ofttimes he falleth into the fire, and oft into the water* (Matthew 17:14–15, emphasis added).

Now this boy had a spiritual need—deliverance. What did Jesus do when He was confronted with this tormented child who was under such a tense level of demon possession that he literally was falling into fire and water? Did Jesus back off from this boy's problems? No way:

And Jesus rebuked the devil; and he [the devil] *departed out of him: and the child was cured from that very hour* (Matthew 17:18, emphasis added).

Jesus spoke the Word and completely turned the boy's circumstances around, and He'll do the same thing for your loved ones too. You can make the difference in your loved ones' lives if you will take them, by faith, to Jesus and receive His transforming power for their situations.

IT'S TIME FOR OUR LOVED ONES TO ARISE

Sometimes when we read about healings or deliverances, the devil may begin to play tricks in our minds. We find ourselves thinking, "Yeah, Jesus may have been able to handle that situation; but it's not nearly as bad as mine." Well, let me show you something that will wipe out all your excuses:

And behold, there cometh one of the rulers of the synagogue, Jairus by name; and when he saw him [Jesus], *he fell at his feet, And besought him greatly, saying, My little daughter lieth at the point of death: I pray thee, come and lay thy hands on her, that she may be healed; and she shall live* (Mark 5:22–23).

Here we see a father named Jairus coming to Jesus on behalf of his deathly sick child. I looked up *Jairus*, and found the name means "He shall enlighten." After his encounter with Jesus, Jairus certainly became enlightened to the transforming pawer of God's Word. He found out that it is never too late for Jesus to tum negative circumstances around.

On His way to heal Jairus' daughter, Jesus stopped to heal a woman who had been hemorrhaging for 12 years. While Jesus was talking to this woman, someone from Jairus' household came and said:

. . . Thy daughter is dead: why troublest thou the Master any further? (Mark 5:35).

Honestly speaking, unless your loved one has died and you are trying to get him resurrected, your problem certainly isn't this bad, is it? I can imagine the utter hopelessness Jairus must have felt when he heard that his precious, young daughter had died. He may have thought, "If we never would have stopped to heal that woman, my daughter would be alive."

However, look at Jesus' reaction. Did He break down and start condemning Himself for not being on time to save the girl? No, He began to encourage this distraught father, "Jairus, I know this looks bad; but just keep hanging on to God's transforming power."

When Wally and I were in Amarillo, Texas as assistant pastors, we were involved in prison ministry. Every Sunday afternoon, we would go and preach in the prisons. Wally would minister to the men and I would minister to the women. One Sunday we had been invited out to dinner by one of the couples in the church. The woman was a new Christian who was just getting ahold of the Word, and her husband was not a Christian; nevertheless, he had come to church with her that Sunday. We accepted their invitation; however, we told them that we would have to leave right after dinner to fulfill our obligation to the prison. Then the woman asked if she and her husband could go with us and watch us minister. We thought it would be strange to have an unsaved person accompany us to a prison service, but the husband wanted to go so we said that it was fine with us.

The woman and I finished ministering first, and we were sitting in the waiting room waiting for Wally and her husband. She said to me, "Marilyn, I know my husband is going to get saved. The Bible says if I believe on the Lord, my house will get saved." She had gotten ahold of God's Word—His transforming power. We had begun to speculate on the different ways that her husband's salvation might come about when the prison chaplain walked in and said, "I've got good news! Pastor Hickey just prayed with your husband and he received the Lord."

It doesn't matter when, where, or how God's Word will begin to transform our situations, does it? The only thing that matters is that God's Word works! What happened when they arrived at Jairus' house? This was such a sad occasion. Jairus' house was full of people, who were weeping and wailing over his daughter:

And when he [Jesus) *was come in, he saith unto them, Why make ye this ado, and weep? the damsel is not dead, but sleepeth* (Mark 5:39, emphasis added).

178

The people began to laugh at Jesus—they thought He was nuts—but it didn't matter to Jesus what they thought. He just made everyone leave the room where the girl was lying, except for His three disciples, Jairus, and his wife:

And he took the damsel by the hand, and said unto her, Talitha cumi; which is, being interpreted, Damsel, I say unto thee, arise (Mark 5:41).

Jesus was saying, "Little lamb, it is getting up time." Doesn't that sound like Jesus? Isn't that just what He would say? Do you remember when your mother used to wake you up when you were little? She'd kiss you and say, "Honey, it's time to get up." Wasn't that just the warmest, sweetest feeling?

What did the young girl do when Jesus spoke the transforming power of God's Word into her spirit:

And straightway the damsel arose, and walked; for she was of the age of twelve years. And they were astonished with a great astonishment (Mark 5:42).

She got up and began to walk around. I can just picture the look of shock on the faces of all those people who had laughed at Jesus. They were probably stunned to silence! Parents, put your faith in God's Word—Jesus. Although your children may be dead in trespasses, sins, and all kinds of garbage, you must not let go of God's transforming power. Whether your children live at home with you or on the other side of the world, one day Jesus is going to say, "Little lamb, little lamb, it's time to rise up out of your sins." And do you know what your little lambs are going to do? That's right, they are going to get up too. So be sure to keep on Satan-proofing your family, and refuse to let go of

179

God's transforming power for their lives.

Just as Jesus told that girl to arise, God is saying to you that it is time for your children to arise out of the defeating lifestyles in which they may be functioning. It's time for them to be transformed into the wonderful vision that God has for them. Did you know that God has made a special promise to fathers concerning their children?

And he shall turn the heart of the fathers to the children, and the heart of the children to their fathers, lest I come and smite the earth with a curse (Malachi 4:6).

Perhaps your relationship with your children has been strained lately, or maybe it is just plain shot! Be encouraged, because this is a day of enlightenment. Your children aren't going down the drain—no matter what might have transpired in the past. From this day forward, we mothers and fathers are enlightened and we are going to learn how to deal with our children.

THE MOTHER'S FAITH

We've been looking at the father's faith; now I want to look at the mother's faith. There is something very unique about a mother's faith. It allows us to give our children the benefit of the doubt despite how bad the situation may appear. We mothers seem to be equipped with some extra mercy concerning our children; we can believe that sooner or later our children are going to come out on top of their circumstances.

The Syrophoenician mother certainly stretched out in supernatural faith on behalf of her hurting daughter:

And, behold, a woman of Canaan came out of the same coasts, and cried unto him, saying, Have mercy on me, O Lord, thou son of David; my daughter is grievously vexed with a devil (Matthew 15:22).

This woman's daughter was demon-possessed. Your children may not be this troubled, but could they be influenced by what they watch on television or the internet? Have you ever monitored the programs that your children like to watch or the video games they play? Do you know what kinds of values they are developing based upon the immoral lifestyles of those characters portrayed on television? Parents need to become more involved with their children so that Satan doesn't pick them off like ducks at a shooting gallery. Your children are your fruit, so make sure that you are protecting them from Satan's influence even in your home.

Looking back on this desperate mother who sought Jesus' help, she said her daughter was grievously vexed. The spirits possessing this girl were hurting her, and she needed to be set free. The devil was hurting that poor girl then, and he is still hurting people today. Living a lifestyle beneath that which God has destined for people hurts! So, the woman came to Jesus:

But he answered her not a word. And his disciples came and besought him, saying, Send her away; for she crieth after us. But he answered and said, I am not sent but unto the lost sheep of the house of Israel (Matthew 15:23–24).

I love this woman's tenacity. She could easily have been offended by Jesus and the disciples and walked away. But instead she came closer and began to worship Jesus. She said, "Lord, help me."

But he answered and said, It is not meet to take the children's bread, and to cast it to dogs. And she said, Truth Lord: yet the dogs eat of the crumbs which fall from their master's table (Matthew 15:26–27).

Jesus actually called her a dog! But did she turn away and run home crying? No! She was determined to get ahold of Jesus Christ, the living Word—God's transforming power—for her daughter! She was not about to let anything stop her, and she got the victory for her daughter:

Then Jesus answered and said unto her, O woman, great is thy faith: be it unto thee even as thou wilt. And her daughter was made whole from that very hour (Matthew 15:28).

Offenses are deliberate traps that have been laid by the devil. If you're not very careful, you'll fall into one of these traps and miss your miracle. Perhaps indignation would be the natural response to some situation, but it's your choice as to whether you are going to operate in the natural (your old nature) or the supernatural (your new nature). The woman Jesus was talking with chose not to become offended by the way Jesus treated her and by the rudeness of His disciples. She chose not to be offended, even when Jesus called her a dog. Rather, she humbled herself and said, "Lord, if I am a dog, I am Your dog and I want the crumbs that fall from Your table."

Years ago, a man with a marvelous, miracle ministry came to our church. He really led a consecrated life and fasted and prayed so much that he looked like a pile of bones. There were always so many miracles when he came, but there also were so many people who were offended by him. Our telephone at the church would ring off the wall with people saying, "He is so crude." And he was. I remember one night he said to a woman, "What are you doing up here tonight? I prayed for you last night. Sit down!" She just kind of crept off and sat down and missed her miracle. But do you know that the people who hung in there and refused to become offended experienced many miracles in their lives?

Now don't get me wrong; I am not saying that this man was right to be so offensive. I don't really know what his problem was, but I do know that the people who allowed his crude personality to cause them to become offended really missed out on their miracles.

POWER TO TRANSFORM THE PAST

The fourth thing I want you to understand is that God's transforming power can correct situations which may have resulted from improper parenting. Let's face it, no matter how good our intentions may be sometimes we parents promote failure in our children rather than faith.

One day my son, Mike, said, "Mother, if you and Dad had put half as much into me as you put into Sarah, I would be much further down the road." I almost responded defensively, "Well, Michael, we tried. But you really botched it up sometimes, and we had a very hard time dealing with you."

But the Lord said, "Don't do that. Don't be defensive at all. Just admit where you blew it." So, instead of reading my son the riot act, I said, "Michael, you're right. There were things that we did wrong. Can you find it in your heart to forgive us?" He said, "Of course I do."

Perhaps you have made some mistakes raising your children. But is God going back on His Word found in Proverbs 11:21 just because you may have blown it? No, because God's transforming power can undo any mistake we may have made in raising our children. Although it was certainly unintentional, I failed my son in some areas; but I never failed to love him. And God has brought Michael through despite my mistakes.

There was a little boy born in Egypt who, if not for his mother's faith, would never have achieved God's goal for his life:

And the woman conceived, and bare a son: and when she saw him that he was a goodly child, she hid him three months (Exodus 2:2).

The Hebrew word for *goodly* can mean "beautiful, prosperous, and excellent;" that's what this baby's mother saw when she looked into his tiny face. All babies are beautiful to their mothers, right? I've never heard a mother say, "I've got the ugliest baby in the world." Have you? The baby may have big ears or a big nose, and most newborns look kind of beat up. But to the mother, that baby is absolutely beautiful.

I don't blame Jochebed one bit for refusing to allow her son to be killed because of some stupid Egyptian law:

And Pharaoh charged all his people, saying, Every son that is born ye shall cast into the river, and every daughter ye shall save alive (Exodus 1:22).

Jochebed really had a mother's faith for her baby. She hid him for three months. Then she put him in an ark and floated him down a river full of crocodiles. The baby finally ended up in Pharaoh's daughter's bathtub. When Pharaoh's daughter drew the baby out of the Nile River, she had compassion on him. She named the baby *Moses*, which means "drawing out," took him home, and raised him as her own son.

Because of his mother's faith, Moses' life was spared; and he was highly educated and had the best of everything. After some really serious learning experiences, Moses, at 80 years of age, answered God's call upon his life to deliver the Israelites out of Egypt.

Looking back on the circumstances surrounding Moses' birth, would you have foreseen all of this in his future? I doubt it. But God's transforming power turned Moses' life around. So, instead of being killed instantly at birth or becoming dinner for a bunch of hungry crocodiles, Moses became the deliverer of Israel.

When we compare Moses' situation to what we may be experiencing, we can say that not all Christian parents were born again at early ages. Some of us spent a lot of years living in sinful lifestyles; and therefore, our children were raised in ungodly homes—they may have had very difficult lives. But regardless of their beginnings, God has plans for your children—they may be future deliverers in the Body of Christ. So, stop feeling guilty about mistakes you may have made in parenting your children. Seek God and repent. Then ask your children to forgive you, and stand on God's Word—His transforming power for their lives.

CATCH THE FAITH VISION

The last thing I want you to consider is catching God's faith vision for your children. Oftentimes, we see reflections of ourselves and our spouses when we look at our children. And that's okay as long as the traits we see are in accord with God's will. However, what happens when we or our spouses have been involved in alcohol abuse, drug addiction, or other debilitating kinds of lifestyles? How about your children? Have you caught a glimpse of God's faith vision? Don't look at what is occurring in the natural; see your loved ones by faith!

I can remember when Mike used to come by the church while he was high on drugs. He was so pitiful. But one day God showed me how to catch His faith vision for my son. I would envision Mike with a Bible in his hands, praising the Lord—just as God saw when He looked at my son. Then one summer night, I saw Mike standing in the back of the church with his hands lifted high in the air, and he was singing in tongues. Praise God! His faith vision had been manifested from the spiritual realm into the natural realm. Hold on to God's transforming power and begin to see what God sees when He looks at your loved ones. God never called believers to be conformers, right? We are here to be transformers so we can subdue the earth as He put us here to do in the first place.

I want you to know that I am praying for every one of you to begin to take authority over your circumstances—that's what God has destined for all people:

So God created man in his own image . . . and God said unto them, Be fruitful, and multiply, and replenish the earth, and subdue it . . . (Genesis 1:27–28).

God does not want your family to become another statistic in the failure-of-the-family epidemic. If you will take the precautions I have been talking about for guarding yourself and your home against Satan's divisive elements, then your family will not give way to the force of his storms. By faith, I am standing with you in prayer. God has commissioned you to be a Satan-proofer; and from this day forward, the devil doesn't have a chance in your home!